Contents

Acknowledgement/Attributions 6

Part I

The Everything that Ever 9

Elders 11

Days things don't work out 12

Exiles 13

Early Lessons in Divine Intent 14

Why my Grandmother Was Like the Roman Empire 15

Daffodils Along the M50 16

Beginnings 17

LifeaChrist 18

When I am Become Again 19

Shopping for Myself 20

For Brother Kennedy 21

Asclepius 22

When I'm Falling 23

Thank you for Holding 24

Part II

OHM 27

Kristallnacht on Late Night Bus 28

Statue Park 29

Times I hear of lives lost 32

Immigrati 33

Honister Crag 34

Visiting Dachau 35

I'm sorry for the Grunts get Killed 37

Kasutori Jidai 38

Lest They Forget 40

In the Museum of Occupation, Riga 42

Little Boy and Tricycle 43

When Mom Goes to War 44

Gravestrips in Sichuan province, West China 45

Oh Come All Ye Trueborn Irishmen 46

Street Demonstration Buenos Aires 49

Part III

The Bookstalls at Stazione Termini, Rome 53

So Where Do You expect to Find Poetry? 55

The Fugitive Muse 59

We're talking Poetry, Right? 61

The Dogs in the Street and Diverse Other Mongrel Clichés 62

On the West Lake, Hangzhou, China 63

Do not Impede Enjambment While the Poet is in Motion 65

Too Much Talk About the Muse 66

How to Succeed at Poetry and make a Lot of Yen 67

OMIGOD Not Another Newgrange Poem 68

His Despairing Friends 70

Especially When 71

How Oft in Spirit Have I Turned to Thee 72

Song of the Wandering Suburbanite 73

Time Will Come There's Nothing left 74

Part IV

TVIVF 77

Towards an Understanding of People who Talk to Themselves 78

An Old Man Makes love 79

IT'S THAT MAN AGAIN! 81

Concerning an Excursion into the RSainforest 83

The Martyrdom of St Andrew 85

Tiler on a Rooftop Above Ujedz, Prague 86

St. Augustine and the Child 87

Is it Possible to be Elegant on a Bicycle in Traffic in the Rain? 88

Inanimates 89

Homage to Maximillian Kolbe 90

Teachers 91

To the memory of Edward Tenison DD 92

The Emperor Advises 94

Bosnian Housewife 95

Annunciations on a Journey Through the Outskirts of Milan 96

And Suddenly the Sun Again

By
Eamonn Lynskey

Seven
Towers

A SEVEN TOWERS PUBLICATION

And Suddenly the Sun Again
First published 2010
By
Seven Towers Agency, 4, St Mura's Terrace,

Strangford Road, East Wall, Dublin 3, Ireland.

www.seventowers.ie

ISBN 978-0-9562033-6-6

Photos and illustrations on pages 8, 26, 52, 76, 100 reproduced as per acknowledgements on page 6; all other photos taken in Bluebell and Inchicore, Dublin 12, Sarah Lundberg, Seven Towers Agency, (c) 2010. Cover photo Sarah Lundberg, Seven Towers Agency, (c) 2010.

Cover, artwork, type and layout design and typesetting by
Seven Towers Agency
www.seventowers.ie

Printed by Genprint, Ireland.
Printed on 90gsm Muncken Bookwove White.

Part V

January and How to Hold Her 101

Hotel Room Easter 102

On Grafton St it's sidling into Summer 103

Elegy for the Philadelphia Wireman 104

Physics Today 105

Gliese 581c 106

Entre Sardana I Sardana 107

Mastermind 109

An Italian Wedding 110

There is an Hour of the Night 111

Springtime at the Zoo 112

First Green Shoots 113

The Dark Side of the Earth 114

Sudden Rainshower 115

ACKNOWLEDGEMENTS

Grateful acknowledgement is given to the following publications where some of these poems have previously appeared:
The Irish Press 'New Irish Writers' (ed. David Marcus); *Cyphers* (Dublin); *Poetry Ireland Review, Orbis* (UK); *Electric Acorn* (Dublin Writers' Workshop); *The Stinging Fly* (Dublin); *The Liffey Valley Champion* (Kildare); *The SHOp Poetry Magazine* (Cork); *Extended Wings* (Rathmines Writers' Group, Dublin); *The Sunday Tribune* 'New Irish Poetry'; *Shades of Scalderwood* (Dublin 15 Writers' Group); *Riposte* (Dublin); *Crannóg* Galway); *Living It* (Dublin); *Revival* (Limerick); *Census The Seven Towers Anthology* (Dublin); *The Stoney Thursday Book* (Cuisle Festival, Limerick).

Grateful acknowledgement also is due to the following competitions in which some of these poems were successful or shortlisted:
Clogh Writers Annual Poetry Competition; Francis Ledwidge Poetry Award; The P.E.A.CE. (Prayer, Enterprise and Christian Effort) 'Poem for Peace' Competition; 'Poetry on the Wall' (South Dublin County Council); 'Scríobh' International Poetry Competition (Sligo); The Sunday Tribune/Hennessy Award; The Strokestown International Poetry Competition.

Acknowledgement also to the 'START' (South Tipperary Arts Centre) Chapbook Competition 2004 which shortlisted a sample of this collection in their Poetry Section

Grateful acknowledgement is also due to the many organisers of Open Mic venues in Dublin, London and elsewhere who, over the years, have given the author the opportunity to deliver these poems on-stage, thereby assisting their development towards something approaching finality.

ATTRIBUTIONS

Photographs on p8 are from the author's family collection; brochure on p26 reproduced with permission of the Museum of Occupation, Latvia; Statue Park picture on pp 26, reproduced with permission of The Memento Park, Budapest, Hungary; Editorial on p 26 reproduced with kind permission of the Buenos Aires Herald, Argentina; map on page 56 reproduced with kind permission of the office of Public Works, Ireland; photograph of Maximillian Kolbe on page 76 reproduced with permission of The Open Door Celbridge, Co Kildare; photograph of St Augustine and Child p 76, reproduced with permission of Bernardino di Betto, detto il Pintoricchio, 'Pala di Santa Maria dei Fossi': predella: (dettaglio) sant'Agostino e il bambino che vuole svuotare il mare; Galleria Nazionale, Umbria. (Soprintendenza Beni Storici Artistici ed Etnoantropologici dell'Umbria - Perugia (Italy) by permission of Soprintendenza Beni Storici Artistici ed Etnoantropologici dell'Umbria - Perugia (Italy); news article on p 100 reproduced with permission of *The Irish Times* (Dublin); picture of work by The Philadelphia Wire Man on p100 reproduced with permission of the Fleischer/Ollman Gallery, Philadelphia, USA.

PART I

". . . voices trapped in syllables echoing out of childhood ."

The Everything that Ever

1

(on viewing The Senior Citizen's Project: "...And Start to Wear Purple" at the Irish Museum of Modern Art, Royal Hospital Kilmainham 1999)

Memory: a crate gets broken open
by a song, a rhyme, or by a slash
of line or splash of colour. Now, nudged off
its shelf, it crashes on this polished floor
and I stand still and watch my childhood spill
around me: Inchicore, the Grand Canal,
The Camac. Every place I was is here:

St Michael's Church and that day after Mass
my mother fell and grazed her knee – the fear
in us to see her crying; how I heard
the people of Keogh's Square were wild, and then
how one of them became my first best friend;
how all our days of playing hide and seek
in Islandbridge Memorial Park were fenced
away from Lutyen's stately towers and fountains,
and how our weary evening journeys home
to Old Kilmainham passed the castle gate
where surely Rumplestilskin lived awaiting
rescue; how I watched late sunlight gild
the window frames of this Royal Hospital -
then soldierless and brooding in dry-rot,
a last resort for ghosts and pasts: discarded
farming tackle, Queen Victoria cast in
bronze, awaiting transportation anywhere.

And memory is this sharp wind busy
in the courtyard, blowing last year's leaves
in circles, prising them from corners, searching
through the crate for bits got lodged *(a shout*
ringed round with sunlight): such a rush of pleasure
followed suddenly, inevitably,
by pain. Everything I am is here.

2

New-mown grass, and once again my head
is filled with smells and sunlight and myself
grown small— Those endless summer afternoons
we built our houses, fortresses and castles
from the grass that lay in fresh-cut mounds
in Islandbridge Memorial Park, my mother
reading romances to keep her mind away
from bills and household worries and away
from him that moment working down the mines
in Lancashire, and his letter that hadn't come.

Letters in the hallway and again
my life reveals itself as rows of drawers,
like those once lined the walls of chemist shops,
each neatly labelled — But these drawers contain
the everything that ever happened to us.
Every label noting year and day
and hour, each drawer awaiting scent or sound
or sight to slip the latch, slide open, yield
the past: late evening and my mother, dark-haired,
sitting with us, reading his letter aloud.

Elders

Faint against the drifting sands
our elders — Silhouetted
on long strands of half-uneasy
sleep, their hands outstretched, their voices
trapped in syllables echoing
out of childhood. Deep

within the coils of dreams
our elders — Moving nightly
where the oil-lamps flickered
in the half-breeze, features
those remembered out of yellowed
photographs. We stir,

we turn, we stumble towards
their whisperings, across the dunes
we've crossed before so often, struggling
towards the rim, the moment when
we feel the final chrism cool
against our skin. And firmer

in the swirling sands our elders
every night that passes, every
night we strain to glimpse
their distant faces, hear
their voices clearer every troubled
sleep that draws them nearer, nearer...

Days Things Don't Work Out

Dromore Wood, Co. Clare

Days things don't work out the way we thought,
we sense we've stumbled into something planned,
something set and programmed all those several
thousand million years and more back
when the stars were only coloured bits
of crystal and the galaxies a twinkling
mix of mortar in His celestial bucket.

So, the day I walked Dromore again
to check if those old paths still lead down
to the lake's edge, if those old rocks
still huddled on the shoreline with the reeds,
He sent His predetermined rains, at first
apologetically in showers because
He knew my need— But sent them, nonetheless.

Inexorable the workings of His will.
Unstoppable tornadoes and tsunamis
sweeping villages away. And those
who say these visitings are punishments
sent because we sink ourselves in sin?—
What care He about our dalliances,
considering the business He's in?

This architectured universe, devised
when there were no requirements to consult
stakeholders nor supply a blueprint— Just
creation of the particles would shape
the earth, the sky, the fire, the water, make
a habitable space. A work in progress
yet— Witness the tectonic plates.

Every leaf that takes the rain reminder
of how much we know, how much we don't,
despite our centuries of trying to peer
over His shoulder. Day we find the answers
day we finally become divine.
And days things don't work out? Abrupt reminder:
that Glorious Day has not as yet arrived.

Exiles

After 'Exiles 1943' by Patrick Hennessy (1915-1981), Dublin Municipal Gallery, and the piano recital given there by Katarzyna Moscicka, May, 2003

This pianist from Warsaw plays Chopin
and Field without a score. And afterwards
I sit again before your picturing
of one who faces out to sea from shore
because I need to search again my scrapbooks
of the past to see if there's a chart
will find the men who shipped to England in
the fifties and found work and lost themselves.

Lost themselves in Lancashire as much
as Chopin did in Edinburgh, Field
in snowbound Moscow, which is just to say
they found themselves as exiles, like this man
you painted with his back to everything
that made him, man who'll spend a few years sending
letters home from colliery towns in Yorkshire,
then less frequently, then nothing. And

because you show him barebacked, shoulders tensed
against the sunlight he reminds me
of my father washing just before
he'd go to play in pubs, without a score,
the jigs and reels he learned in Manchester -
Reminds me of him waiting for the mailboat,
silent, suitcase at his feet, his mind
already past the pier at Holyhead.

No score will guide the hand that cannot play.
No brush the mind from which no colours long
to pour. Not what was there before them but
the music that they brought filled out the years
of concert halls or drinking houses. Ghosting
through her fingers here my father, Field
and Chopin, and the one you pictured standing,
back turned, facing outwards. Exiles.

Early Lessons in Divine Intent

(Young people, evening, Clonsilla Road)

When I was young, and stumbling towards myself
and finding how to fit my tongue to words,
I learned to call them 'mongols', those strange people
my grandmother said were touched by God
and sent among us to recall our loss
when Adam's knowledge cost us Paradise.

Those early faces held for me no trace
of Ghengis Khan, nor all his race that over-ran
an empire. But my post-war picture-books
incited hate of suicidal Japs
who Zero-dived American Destroyers,
screaming warcries out of angled cockpits.

I suffused those narrowed eyes with evil
until, years later, old war-footage woke
in me a raging hurt for those who drank
the ritual libation, tied the scarf
around their temples, told the sacred prayer,
ascended their irrevocable skies.

And now this evening all my childyears burst
their casements where they've long been stored,
to spill out on the road before me crayons,
slate-boards clean of chalk and broken toys
made whole again and those first meanings
of first words, clear and sharp.

And down the path they come, my long-lost 'mongols',
flooding out from forests now they've heard
my wars are done and I am home again
among her words intended kindly to describe them.
In woollen caps they come, their voices bright
like birds, each one an earnest of God's plan

to people out a colony in space
where man, made in His image, would exist
in innocence, with stars and moon and sun
suspended in the firmament as lanterns
for his day and night, and Providence
supply the needs of simple, deathless life.

Why My Grandmother Was Like
The Roman Empire

My grandmother was like the Roman Empire
in the way she would accumulate
all forms of deity and divinity —
The fruit of her innumerable forays
into Devotions and Retreats. And like

the Romans and their temples that they filled
from far and wide she was unconcerned
with incongruities — A Virgin Mary
bought a year ago would suddenly be
dwarfed by a monster Child of Prague. As did

the Emperors bring back from barbarous lands
new gods, so too each mission week
another picture of The Sacred Heart
would be enshrined, despite the many gathered
on her mantelpiece already. And —

despite the obvious imbalances
of stature (real and divine) within
this ever-growing plaster congregation —
this curiously lop-sided combination
of church history and imagination

didn't trouble her. Like the Romans,
she had no fixed beliefs, although
she had a fondness for St. Martin who,
she told me, had been helpful in a matter
years ago, and so she always placed him

out front in the row between St. Clare
and Padre Pio, beside Himself. This stark
hierarchical confusion didn't bother
the Romans. My Grandmother neither. She held, that if
there *is* a God (which there must be, she said)

He's big enough to keep the rest in order.
These might be got to intervene, but God
is God and therefore unassailably supreme,
my grandmother argued. And the Romans,
with their Pantheon of divers gods, agreed.

Daffodils Along the M50

I never see the daffodils line up
along the motorway but I remember them
that day I drove to work distraught
because I'd phoned the week before to say
I'd call to see you sometime soon, but didn't.

They deck the highways every year I think
to tell us something good about ourselves—
despite all evidence to the contrary:
our day-to-day dishonesties, deceits,
our unintended cruelties, neglects.

And every year they tell us to keep close
our friends because we do not know the day,
the hour they will be thieved away, and we
be left alone with those to whom our stay
or passing is a matter of small moment.

Beginnings

Remembering Mrs Mary O'Keeffe,
of Crusheen, Co .Clare

When their school photographs arrived
was when I heard the door swing closed. The flowers,
the Mass, the graveside prayers and handshakes all
had passed me by as necessary rituals
somehow unconnected with your absence.
Even during the family conversations
in your kitchen after the Month's Mind
I thought I'd heard you somewhere in the background
busy with the tea-things and the cake
you would have ordered from Clarke's for the occasion.

But look at these two bright, resplendent faces,
fearless, and ready to take on the world
and all its works and pomps — And I forgot,
and took an envelope and wrote your name
to send this photograph to you because
I knew you'd want to sit and look at them
a long time, these great-grandchildren,
these extraordinary envoys to a future
you (and I) will never know. And then
the door-latch clicked in place and I remembered.

It's times like these the heart discovers room
for ancient certainties — A Life Hereafter,
peopled out with favourite relatives
and friendly saints. I'd even credit Charon
and his raft across the Styx if he
allowed me to believe that you could see them,
these young warriors, armed with innocence,
and striking out to unknown territories.
We must make the best of our beginnings—
Soon enough the gods reveal their plans.

The LifeaChrist

(Religious Education, Dublin, c. 1963 AD)

Take out your LifeaChrists and open up
page 49 I think... Yes, 49...

I see a lot of people there without
their LifeaChrist in front of them. Where's yours?
And you. Where's your LifeaChrist? — Right!
Seasagaí suas na daoine who forgot
their LifeaChrists. There's no excuse: we've done it
every Monday since September. You —
Where's your LifeaChrist? Oh, you forgot?
You FORGOT? Tar amach anseo —
Sín amach do lámh. **! !**
Now maybe you'll remember next Monday?

Tusa? Cúis gáire agat, an ea? Tar anseo.
Lámh amach. **! !** ... noimead ...
Lámh eile. **! !** Suigh síos.

Now you. Your LifeaChrist ? **! !**
Pure and simple thoughtlessness. And you?—
O, you! Do I remember you forgot
your LifeaChrist last Monday too? Do lámh:
! ! And you? **! !**
Now. Suigh síos gach éinne. And don't anyone
come in again without their LifeaChrist.
Right! Open up page... yes, page 49,
and those who have no LifeaChrists themselves
look into the LifeaChrist beside you. We
were on the second paragraph... Yes
the second paragraph. 'Jesus teaches us
the need for mercy'. Tusa ansin— Read!

(Author's note: *The exclamation mark [!] in bold type represents the smack of
the leather strap on the hand of the child*)

When I am Become Again

(remembering a teaching colleague
Jean-Louise Pech)

When I am become again
the furniture of the universe,
my several entrails, teeth and tongue
at one with roots and lichen, all
the hurried turmoil of my days
dispersed, my marrow mixed with clays
and chandlers, all my molecules
restructured into rains: become again

will I be when, mere artefact
of nature's whim, my stomach muscles
decompose to rainbows, all
my sinews stretch in stellar space,
my eyelash frets an insect wing,
my breath is caught in April winds
that trouble swollen lakes, that shake
the yellow scent from daffodils.

When I am become again ethereal,
my memories meshed with moistures
I will to look for you, my friend — these
many years a gleam along Orion's sword,
whose laughter I've heard often
in the eaves at night. These,
my particles, far-scattered into twig
or stone or star, will seek you out.

Shopping for Myself

In the late night supermarket I go shopping
for myself. I'll have that pound of liver,
yes, and lights and kidney, please. And yes,
that bit of smoked lung too. That bit
of brain is all you've left? That heart so reddened
with anxieties and pinned with sprigs
of plastic sympathy? Wrap up the lot.

It's at the liquor counter we meet up
in that big mirror with the whiskey ads:
myself and me - friends of course - but quarrelsome
over brands and strengths and whether or not
a few cigars. I hate his guilts, his slouch,
his waiting every week among the stacks
of vodka my inevitable arrival.

In the late night supermarket I go shopping
for myself, but - if I can - avoid him
standing there so righteous in between
the cup-a-soups and powdered sauces. But
he always spots me, beckons. It's no use
examining the cereals, pretending
not to see him, or trying to escape—

he stands there with that irritating smile
suggesting he knows something I don't know
about myself— but sucks to him. I know
my time is running out. It's no big secret.
Hmmm: What's this? A Special Super Offer
on the cans of Bass and Smithwicks? Yes,
I'll take a dozen more. I love to

For Brother Kennedy

(Teacher of 6th Class, St James Christian Brothers
Primary School, 1962)

Embalmed within the casket of my mind
your face still keeps its leathered cheek intact
and thrusting back the winding sheet, stern
and resurrect, you stand beside me now
that I have stepped beyond the midday-break,
and pause to settle texts for final classes.

Events and intervening paths, things done
and seen since last we met have coalesced,
become as blurred as pages flivelled back -
your habit when you'd question us, and then
reveal the answer caught in flight, a word pinned
tight beneath your thumb. Again your classroom

wraps me in its smells of creosote floors
with knots and nailheads, rickety ink-stained desks
and clothes damp after rain. Like you I break
the chalk inside my fist. Like you I watch
my class out of the comer of my eye,
my hand splayed on the board is your hand placed

against the easel lest it swing away. Like
mediaeval saint, skin stretched yet
uncorrupt, you have begun to drape
your black soutane around my shoulders, pockets
full of slips of praise and admonition,
precepts underlined with patience, kindness.

Asclepius

(The big chief medicine man of the ancient Greeks)

Asclepius taps his keyboard, views my life
in scrolls. I smooth my toga, cast my eye
around his medical paraphernalia:
blood-pressure gauge (quite often), adjustable bed

(sometimes), his stethoscope (innumerable),
that oxygen mask (not once, thank Jupiter!),
that weird-looking machine for something-or-other
in the corner — "We need to look at this." It's '*WE*'—

A joint attempt to thwart the Cruel Fates,
Asclepius and me, our staffs in hand,
Hippocrates alongside and the snake
our symbol— "Yes, you'd better check this out".

It's *YOU*. That is, it's *ME* again. Disease
is a single seat, one way. Asclepius pauses,
writes a name. "I'll send you to this man.
The best there is." The Delphic Oracle?—

I do *not* say. Sarcastic jokes? No, not
a good idea with one's GP. Outside
it's raining and the temple steps are treacherous.
There's my neighbour Julius now going in

to cast his lots, to have his history
of physical disintegration flashed up
on the screen. And he, so stooped and pale
and thin — "Yo, Julius! You're looking well!"

At least I don't look half as bad as him.

When I'm Falling...

Never noticed him before sitting,
grinning in the corner of my life—
Lately he's been standing up more,
moving around and looking at his watch.

These first impairments of the eye, the ear —
The growing clutter of pills and ointments — Futile
armoury he finds hilarious. Well,
he's entitled to — Considering

the nervous search for signs each morning— Such
dark lines, such saggings of the jowl, such
weariness of limb— And look! There
he is again beside the bed, beckoning.

My eyes are everywhere these days in case
he bursts a paper bag behind me, or jumps
suddenly from behind a door! The tricks
that he can pull! No, never noticed him

so much before, but now it's cat and mouse
between us, we're like David and Goliath
(but no sling). Or rather, we're like two
prizefighters circling the ring, the one

so full of confidence, the other sweating,
desperate for the bell. Or it's like I'm on
a window ledge forty storeys up
and waiting for the final push... Enough

of fancy imagery. Thing is: When
I'm plunging towards the Void can I deny him
total victory?— I have a plan:
When I'm falling, I will close my eyes...

Thank You For Holding

Because statistics tell me
that you'll see me out, my love,
I would be much obliged
if you would grant me this
one last request: Before

the lid is fastened, please
insert between my prayerful fingers
and my rosary beads
my mobile phone
and please make sure

that for the next few days, at least,
YOURS is
(a) in credit,
(b) fully charged,
(c) turned on, and not

(d) buried at the bottom of your handbag
where it is liable to dial out during
a search for car-keys, spectacles,
credit-cards, lipstick, and et cetera
(a full list available on request). And

if you do not hear from me
during the mournful days
sequential to my demise I pray
you put aside your inconsolable grief
and give me a call. And

please be patient as I
may have some difficulty
in coming to the phone.
Thank you for holding.
Your call could be important to me.

PART II

"There is a wall in Galway runs beside the Via Ostiense leading out of Rome"

THE OCCUPATION MUSEUM WAS
ESTABLISHED IN RĪGA IN 1993 BY
THE OCCUPATION MUSEUM
FOUNDATION (OMF) to

show what happened to Latvia, its land and people under
two occupying totalitarian regimes from 1940 to 1991

remind the world of the crimes committed by foreign
powers against the state and people of Latvia

remember the victims of the occupation: those who
perished, were persecuted, forcefully deported or fled the
terror of the occupation regimes.

Exhibit hall.

MUSEUM EXHIBITS

Visitors are introduced to the fifty one-years of occupation of
Latvia (1940–1991) in terms of the first Soviet occupation
(1940–1941), the National Socialist German occupation
(1941–1944/45), followed by the second Soviet occupation
(1944/45–1991).

Historical documents,
artifacts and pictures
show the impact of two
totalitarian regimes on
Latvia as a state and na-
tion. Personal keepsakes
testify to oppression and
persecution, but also to
defiance and resistance, to
inhumane conditions in
prisons and Siberian exile,
but also to the strength of
the human spirit in
extreme adversity.
Museum texts and
explanations are provided
in Latvian, English, German
and Russian.

Aluminium cup from a forced
labour camp in Karaganda, Kazakhstan.

Buenos Aires Herald
Founded in 1876

Senior Editor: Andrew Graham-Yooll
Executive Editor: Michael Soltys
Managing Editor: Dan Krishock

The remains of memory

The announcement last Friday in Buenos Aires of the identification of the bones of Mrs Azucena Villaflor de De Vincenti, one of the founders of the Mothers of Plaza de Mayo protest movement created in April 1977 to find their "disappeared" children, was almost lost amid the reports on the aftermath of the terrorist bombs in London. Locally, the imminent announcement by Mrs Duhalde of her decision to run for a Senate seat against Mrs Kirchner who had made a similar self-proclamation the day before — and got herself swamped by the coverage given the London bombings — also helped to push the discovery of the remains of Villaflor and two other women into a secondary place. However, the discovery should be recovered as a major landmark in Argentina's acknowledgement of a memory that many people would prefer to forget. Azucena Villaflor, Esther Ballestrino de Careaga and María Ponce de Bianco, whose bones were found in an unmarked grave in General Lavalle, were among the women, and men, snatched over three days after an initial raid on the Holy Cross church on December 8, 1977. The name most associated with that series of abductions of unarmed women and men by heavily armed thugs who first stormed the church meeting hall is that of the naval officer turned sinister monster, Alfredo Astiz. In just a few months of organized protest, a group of middle aged women demanding to know where their missing offspring were being held by the regime had become a threat to tyrants, or so they were perceived by the plainclothes troops that stormed the church premises.

The identification of those bones is obviously important for the families of the women because while the names are remembered in a plaque at the church on Urquiza street, and in a street name in Puerto Madero, the relatives now have some remains to mourn. The remains thus become more important as a real testimony of a past that is slipping away with too many questions still unanswered. The bones are a silent statement resounding down the years which many Argentines still refuse to hear.

Whether we like it or not, the announcement of the identification of the remains of the three women in Buenos Aires fitted with the report of the horror in London. While the British public were mourning the victims of one form of terror, Argentines should have felt reminded of their own local brand of state terror which, 27 years after the abduction of Villaflor, still demands the awareness necessary to prevent repetition.

FEGYVERBE!
FEGYVERBE!

OHM

"Sir? Yes, back row, left... Just hold for the mic
a moment, if you will... Yes, sir? ... ...
—ohm— it's a multilayered process.
—ohm— the particularities of each instance
—ohm— permutate. Permutate
—ohm— even as events are still
in progress. —ohm— But yes, we might have been
—ohm— better prepared for the eventuality
—ohm— that came about. —ohm— Yes,
something programmatic like this, —ohm—
that is to say —ohm— something planned
—ohm— could've have been, —ohm— should've been
—ohm— quantified in terms of risk,
strategic out-comes, types of ordnance. Yes
—ohm— I would agree with you, yes. —ohm—
Yes, that would seem now, —ohm—
would now be seen as a preferred scenario
—ohm— and —ohm— we regret,
as always in these combat situations
—ohm— we regret collateral damage
anywhere it happens. —ohm— As regards
the numbers you have mentioned, sir —ohm—
regarding civilian casualties —ohm—
we have no official information yet to hand
So —ohm— I cannot comment on —ohm—
I am unable to confirm or deny
—ohm— the figures you have mentioned. —ohm—
Except to say that —ohm— —ohm— reports
of civilian casualties are probably
—ohm— exaggerated. —ohm— Yes, sir.
Yes, sir... well, I am trying to give you answer...
Well, if you will allow me... Thank you, sir...
—ohm— Yes, there are some reports
of children, of child casualties. —ohm—
unconfirmed as yet —ohm— —ohm—
Sir, if you will allow me... Sir,
I am trying to answer... Sir... Thank you, sir.
—ohm— As soon as —ohm— Immediately
we receive reports from commanders in the field
   [a note is passed to the officer from behind]
—ohm— a decision will be made —ohm—
as to whatever investigations are needed
—ohm— into the concerns raised —ohm—
Thankyouladiesandgentlementhat
concludesthemilitarybriefingfortoday".

Kristallnacht on the Late Night Bus

When thugs fell out among themselves upstairs
on the late-night bus from town I knew then
why it was that everyone kept quiet
when the cattle trucks went rumbling past, full —
and quieter still when they came back later, empty.

And when threats ran out and knives were drawn
and two drunks fought together in the aisle
I knew then how it was that people bought
the children's clothes, and shoes were put on sale
outside the camps; how uniformed gangsters

ruled the streets at will and forced old men
to scrub the kerbs before they smashed their heads.
When bottles smashed across the chromium bars
and showered their brittle specks of coloured glass
across the heaving floor the blood froze

in our faces and the only thing
that any one could wish for at that moment
and above all else this world might offer
was just one clear run across the aisle
and down the swaying staircase. When the bus

lurched sideways to a halt and all the louts
gave up their enmities to fight against
whatever representative of law
had come to tackle them - what could match
our abject, coward relief? What kristallnacht

could match our terror on that late-night bus
from town when seats were ripped apart and who
dared look was spat on? Deep within we felt
the stir of something sharp and forked, a thing
to paralyse a thought, a thing to stop the heart.

Statue Park

Budapest, District XXII

For long I'd wondered where and how I'd mourn
my communist past (the Berlin Wall had seen off
'if and 'whether'): all those drinking sessions
after the Ard Fheis in Liberty Hall,
proudly wearing the stick-on Party Badge -
The Plough and the Stars on a red background - turning
our city swords into ploughshares, our pints of porter
into piss. For long I'd wondered where

and how I'd mourn those wet evenings flogging
the Party Paper around the housing estates,
and those Saturdays spent in the HQ
being lectured to on the Party Policy
on local authority autonomy and the need for a cumann
on every street and then the obligatory talk
on the Evils of Capitalism while we sat secure
and saintly in self-righteous dignified boredom.

I'd often wondered how I'd mourn those mornings
I awaited the arrival of the Party TD
on his non-election visit to the hall-doors
of the dispossessed, thereby showing his interest
extended far beyond mere vote-getting —
And those nights spent wading through as much
of Marx and Engels I could take without
forgetting the bits I'd read the night before.

I'd wondered how I'd mourn those arguments
about farmers getting away with murder [sic]
and driving around in big cars, and living
off the backs of ordinary decent workers [sic]
who paid their taxes and had barely enough
to live on ("TAX the GREEDY, Not the NEEDY!!!") -
And those rounds and rounds of applause for the delegates
who brought fraternal greetings from North Korea.

And then that summer when I was filling out
the visa form for the U.S. Embassy
and came to the box that asked me: 'Have You Ever
Been A Member Of A Communist Party?' — and writing:
'No'. Because, you see, we called ourselves
a Socialist Party. 'Socialists', because
in Catholic Ireland 'socialists' didn't have horns,
forks and tails, unlike the Communists

who tortured priests and spat on Our Lord's picture,
made fun of the Virgin Birth, and did appalling
things to nuns. Because, you see, Ireland
was praying continually for the conversion of Russia, and we
(the socialists) were waiting for the Red Dawn
to break across the concentrated masses
of large industrial urban conurbations -
Then, we would declare our true credentials.

Here in this Statue Park on Budapest's
grey outskirts I have found at last the place
to mourn all that, among the monuments
that once kept watch from public squares and bridges,
hands upraised, their faces set against
the crimes of exploitation and oppression,
features cast in strict accordance with
the dictates of the Central Cultural Committees

of the Cultural-Political and Ideological Forums
of the Fourth International. Walk with me a while
in Statue Park, in Budapest, this day
the Autumn sun is softening the edges
of these megaliths that ringed my youth,
this strange assemblage of young Heroes of
the Soviet Union, and Old Demagogues
haranguing still their vanished multitudes.

Here is Vladimir Illych - not the boy
who saw his brother executed, not
the revolutionary who turned Russia
upside-down - In Statue Park, still stern
and oversized, his frockcoat billowing out,
he stands now shorn of myth: now just a man,
like any other man, his arm raised, maybe
calling help (?), or flagging down a cab (?).

Here too that huge gargantuan monster made
by Istvan Kiss, still striding off his plinth,
with muscles no man ever had, with banner
flying overhead like banner never
flew, his sightless eyes still staring out
across the serried ranks of Party Workers
marching past, his silent roar still rising:
'Arms! To Arms!' as he takes their massed salute.

And here's a plaque was rescued from the rabble:
Janos Asztalos who died defending
Party Headquarters on that fateful day
Hungarians were murdered in the streets.
Here too the tyrant they hacked down, broke-up
and mutilated, then saw resurrected
when the streets were emptied and things were back
to 'normal' and the bodies in the clay.

For long I'd wondered where and how I'd mourn
my communist past, the plough, the stars, the hammer
and the sickle, all those endless meetings
spent in damp rooms planning leaflet-
drops and wrestling with Gestetner printers,
making placards wouldn't run in rain -
Now here in Statue Park I think maybe
I can leave my ghosts behind me. But

these statues stand like sentries on the borders
of my consciousness, and this despite
the everything that's happened. Though I leave them
here I know they'll travel with me. In
the reservoirs of my past the May Day crowds
still march, still sing the 'Internationale',
as the coach pulls out and Lenin, Stalin, Haman,
Bela Kun grow smaller and smaller in the distance.

Times I Hear of Lives Lost

('35 miners die in Ukraine coal mine fire near Kiev',
'25 coal miners killed in north-eastern China' - News reports)

Times I hear of lives lost
underground I hear again
the iron cage clang shut, I hear
you telling of the fear that struck

the heart each time the cables tightened
overhead. Again, I see you
and your fellow colliers
descend through levelled ages, faces

grey with dust no razor gleaned,
no water cleaned -I feel the pick
and shovel cramped against your jacket,
helmet clamped against your skull.

* * *

At home on holidays you puzzled
over diagrams I'd made
at school until suddenly you laughed.
"Why, dammit! That's a Davy Lamp!"

Two weeks of holidays and then
the suitcase in the hallway, then
the letters stamped in Manchester
or mining towns in Wales. Some nights

I see you climb from my dark reservoir
of loss, your shoulders cloaked with coal dust,
lamp in hand. I always call
to you. You always turn away.

Immigrati

*There is a wall in Galway runs beside
the Via Ostiense leading out of Rome...*

This morning on the Via Ostiense
ice is everywhere and they stand huddled
close together at the cross roads, wrapped
in a fog of breath and cigarette smoke:
"Immigrati," you remark, releasing
into second gear. And I recall
a photograph of strong-faced lads, and girls
in shawls lined up against a wall in Galway.

"Vengono qui. From Poland. Yes, they work.
But many. Far too many." Sparks flick
from their fingers as a lorry slows
and they surge forward, shoulders squared like those
who stood that day unsure if they should laugh
or look away, that day the camera froze
their bodies braced for hire, their faces raw,
their eyes fixed warily on the stranger.

In the rear-view mirror they grow smaller
but I see a boy jump from the tailboard,
hear his voice slice through the frosted air:
"Tu, e tu, e tu. No, basta! Basta
cosi". And they fall back again. "It's hard," -
negotiating corners carefully -
"One day a man came to my door: 'Signora,
please. I work for you.'" I see them

lining up again, so many dots
along the Via Ostiense. "Families
too... so hard... Allora...Poverini..."
and your voice breaks as the lorry
passes. They sit talking, gesturing,
and I recall those youngsters standing, smiling
at the camera, a change of clothes,
a bite to eat tied up around their waists.

*There is a wall in Galway runs beside
the Via Ostiense leading out of Rome*

Honister Crag

Cumbria. Slate quarried since 1750s.

Here's to all the men who hacked green slate
from out of Honister Crag and hauled it up
like pack mules on their backs, sweating,
straining, doing what they had to do
to pile the profits for their owners. And
like Sisyphus no sooner one load up
but down again to strain and sweat and hack
the rock 'till injury maim or old age

set them free. This is where their world
began and ended. Brace the frame now,
shoulder up another load— Today
another day of wind and rain and mist
and drizzle, water spitting everywhere,
but I don't have to split out slate from these
unpitying crags, my back is not deformed
by weight of stone. Here in the visitors' centre

men and boys smile out from that one day,
that one sunlit day they posed, all ragged,
happy, or at least content, relieved
for one brief moment from back-breaking toil.
They came to work on Monday, food and 'personals'
slung across their shoulders, slept the nights
billeted together until Friday,
and then home again. Or spent their money

foolishly — The owner's son one Sunday
found Mad Jack McKay in town without
a penny — "Any chance of a subsist,
Gov?"— "Not an earthly". But he spun him
half-a-crown and warned him not to be late
next day. This unaccustomed kindness blinks
out of the darkness, a tiny animal,
rare, unused to light. For here is where

the world ended for these men who strained
and hacked and sweated. Here, on Honister,
is where they had for free these scenic views
we tourists have to pay for now, these views
of winding roads they climbed each week. And here
the sheds they lived in. Here, their photographs.
Their stone memorials: rejected slates
piled up in thousands, overgrown with weeds.

Visiting Dachau

The wind is singing in the wire at Dachau
and whipping up the gravel in the square.
What song is this the wind sings in the wire
at Dachau? And are there words?

A thriving town, famous for
its industry and commerce

Coloured pictures of a prosperous town
with men and women busy, centuries bound
devoutly to commercial life, decent
men and women who work hard, respect
the laws and raise their young in love of order,
industry and quality of product. And
beyond the town the road that leads beyond
the coloured pictures and the words - But these
are not the words the wind is singing in the wire.

A short bus journey to
a place of historical interest

The road leads out beyond the solid buildings
and the intersections and the trams that clang
on corners and the statues of forgotten
worthies and the parks where mothers walk
their children and at last - The railway sidings,
high perimeter fencing and the watchtowers
squatting watching as we pass and talk
dies out because there is this plaint, this sound
of pleading in the wire and we are listening
for the words as if we know there must
be words and we must hear them.

Meet at the main gate in one hour
and please stay with the group

Here, the skeletal outlines of the huts
that housed the damned. And here, the ovens
rusted open, bolts the colour of congealed blood.
And here the showers, echoing our silence. Here,
the square where history cast the die again
and spelled the fates of those who do and those
to whom is done and wind whips up the gravel
at our feet, each pebble round and rattle-hard,
a kind of syllable, but not a word.

This is the museum
No photography please

Instruments and sacks of human hair
and photographs: a naked man submerged
in freezing water while a scientist checks
a gauge; emaciated figures on a cart
were forced to serenade a friend who stumbles
towards a rope; six gypsies in a line
with shaven heads before an officer
who taps his pistol on his thigh and smokes
a cigarette. Behind me someone starts to cry,
but softly, like the wind is whispering outside.

Please resume your seats
on the bus as soon as possible

There was a place where children's shoes were sold
each week and mothers came to buy and asked
no questions. Are there words to tell how mothers
came each week to buy and asked no questions?
Are there words to tell how men and women lived
nearby and did not ask about the trains that passed
each night so full and came back empty? Words
to tell the sound of crying? Words to tell
the shift of gravel in the square? To tell the cries
of someone dying? Words to fit this song
the wind sings in the wire? There must be words.

Thank you for your co-operation.
Please remain seated on the return journey

There are no words to fit this song the wind
sings in the wire, but Dachau names the sounds:
The door slammed open - Dachau! -
The boot slammed into rib - Dachau! -
Soldiers marching over gravel - Dachau! Dachau!
Short abrupt command and volley - Dachau!

This is the song the wind sings in the wire
and Dachau names the sounds but not
the words, because there are no words.

I'm Sorry for the Grunts Get Killed

I'm sorry for the grunts get killed, blown up
or shot in the face in downtown Baghdad,
Mosul, or Basra or whatever place
in occupied Iraq the Emperor
has sent his legions to bring order to the world
with tanks, gunships and Pax Americana.

I'm sorry for young soldiers who stop cars
and find their lives are stopped forever. And
the way their colleagues — caught on videocamera —
come scrambling to collect their twisted bits
of intestine and bladder off the ground
and try to push them back inside again.

'Sorry'. Such a word! The word I use
to squeeze past someone on the bus or when
I accidentally drop a teaspoon. But
I want a word won't sound 'poetic'. Won't
turn this into another formulaic
anti-war tirade, laying blame,

demanding peace. I'm sorry for the mothers
and the wives who lift the phone or get
the telegram or whatever way
it's broken to them. It must be the end
of everything. And then the airport, funeral
out to Arlington, or wherever. In

the catalogue of tortures every Iraqi
man, woman, child has had to suffer
since the legions came I know the deaths
of legionaries will count for little. Still,
I'm sorry for the grunts get killed, their bodies
burned, their charred limbs held up as trophies.

'Kasutori Jidai'

from 'The days of Cheap Liquor'. A photographic record
of Tokyo made by Tadahiko Hayashi in 1946.

Another early morning out with camera
and accoutrements, he walks the streets
of Edogawabashi where he finds
a man intently eating, plate in hand,
where two end-walls have collapsed against each other,
forming a tight triangle. Tadahiko
checks his angles, and the man ignores him,
all his concentration on his food.

Shortly afterwards he finds two boys
in Ueno, filthy ragged urchins sitting
cross-legged at the roadside with a mug
of kasutori shared between them, one
with face screwed up around his cigarette
his eye closed tight against the smoke, the other
waiting for his turn, and naked save
a dirty cloth around his skeletal loins.

In Takadanobaba he has stumbled
over shrub and weed and picked his way
through shattered masonry before he sees
a woman searching in the blackened remnants
of her home. But then before he nears her
she picks up her child and hurries off. But
Tadahiko catches her wild glance,
her hurried frightened snatching at the child.

At Mijake-Zaka, children scramble
in the rubble, circle him with laughter,
questions, voices high and shrill above
the barking dogs. Tadahiko laughs
with them and tries to answer everything
and show them how the world looks through the lens,
while all the time he makes his angles quickly,
knowing children never stay still for long.

That evening when he clipped them up to dry—
his beggars, bars and brothels, demobbed soldiers,
blank-faced people walking cratered roads—
And when he stood as usual judging, balancing,
did his eye keep coming back to Mijake-Zaka
and its laughing children? And the way
their faces filled his frames and blotted out
the twisted metals and the broken walls?

Lest They Forget

Japanese War Commemoration Ceremonies,
August 2005. As Seen On TV

They've had a hard time this month, the Japs,
with all their commemoration ceremonies
of the day we nuked them (I don't mean you and me
of course — I mean 'Western Civilisation').
Endless TV shots of ancient women
carrying flowers through parking lots to lay
at cemetery altars with flickering candles
and photos of the people we sent up in smoke.

Then the pictures of the Mushroom Cloud
That Freed the World - It's hard for them to have it
burst again each year (it's hard for us
as well, considering Ahmadinejad)
but look at what we did for them immediately
afterwards, their skins in shreds. The notes
we took! If ever we need to nuke again,
the medical after-care will be so much better.

Then the TV ads for orange juice
and tasty salads and how not to drown
in shallow water and. It's back to the Land
of the Rising Sun and more commemorations:
The Ending of the War and how we won it.
The pictures of the Emperor in top hat
and tails on that American destroyer,
signing up to end his reign as God.

Then still more pictures: soldiers flogged and tortured,
hanged and butchered — How they brutalised
our boys to build that bridge on the River Kwai—
Horrible! Horrible! (Great movie, though!). And now
I just found out from TV how they murdered
all those Chinese women long before
Our War began! And that's what's really great
about commemoration ceremonies:

They don't let things die down! It's not enough
the Japanese say they're sorry for all that happened.
It's a Bloody Good Thing we nuked them when we did
and they should be reminded every year
of all the things we did to help them up
again despite the terrible things they done
on us. And on those Chinese women. Yes,
we should remind them yearly. Lest they forget.
Otherwise, what hope for peace and love?

In the Museum of Occupation, Riga

What do they teach us, these museums? — This
display in Riga – part of a wooden billet
where they slept twenty to a shelf
made wide enough for ten. You see. You touch.
You try to comprehend their misery, you —
Who never suffered anything like this.

It's like you're in a vast aquarium
watching sharks through glass as thick as several
coats of time and when they dart at you,
you start away and laugh — "It's like as if
it's real!" you say. Well no, it's not, you —
Who never felt those teeth tear out your spine.

Twenty to a shelf was made for ten,
and if you tumbled out to defecate,
then someone on the floor took up your place
so you stayed wrapped in your filth all night. Read
the labels, try to smell the stench, you —
In your clean shirt and brand-new holiday shorts.

How can they reach us, these museums? — Next morning
when you woke you stood in line to shake
the faeces from your ragged clothing into
an open vat (It's all written on a plaque).
Can you hear the plop and splash? You —
Who never woke to anything like that.

Little Boy and Tricycle

(after an exhibit in the Hiroshima Peace Memorial Museum)

He was playing on his tricycle,
the little boy, with all that skill and deftness
only known to three-year-olds when
everything went white, he fell, the pedals
spun, he started crying, didn't stop
until late into evening when he died.

His father summoned all the strength he had
to bury him in the garden he had loved
because (he thought) so small, he would be lonely
for his family, and because so much
was chaos all around then— Iron bridges
buckled, bottles melted out of shape.

And with the small remains he buried too
the tricycle his boy had loved to ride
each morning in the garden, prayed the gods
would let him play with it because (he thought)
him being such a very little boy -
What would be the harm in the Land of Shades?

He never spoke again about the morning
everything went white, endured the pain
for nearly thirty years and then came back
to find the small but neatly-formed frame,
performed the prayers of ritual re-interment
with his ancestors, this time without

the tricycle, rust-encrusted from
its years of travelling the clay, because
(he thought) his spirit now must be as old
as was his father's that day everything
went white— Because (he thought) the boy, become
now venerable shade, no longer needs it.

*(Author's note: 'Little Boy' was the codename given by the
American military to the atom bomb dropped on Hiroshima)*

When Mom Goes to War

(Title of a 'Time' magazine cover story, 2003)

When we hanged that girl of eighteen years
because she wore the uniform of the Reich,
had maimed and killed so many in the camp—
How we reviled her, said: "You don't expect it

from a woman. Yes, the Amazons
who sliced their breasts off better to employ
the spear. But usually, you know... a woman..."
And that other one who made the lampshades

from the tattooed skins in Buchenwald? —
Unnatural. You couldn't call them 'women'.
That was then. This time it's different: Mary
must lay down the body of her Son,

stop supplicating mercy on side-altars,
exchange her blue and white for camouflage
and shoulder on the ammunition belt,
('They hate our freedoms! Bring 'em on!')

This is the New World Order: Moms with guns.
And Moms with smiles and V-for-victory signs
above the bodies of Iraqi prisoners.
Slice the breasts. Let loose the bitches of war.

Gravestrips in Sichuan Province
West China

Along the edges of the fields the gravestrips,
with their headstones marking final destination,
journey's end. And from this speeding train

each strip appears a moment only, then
is whipped away — apt metaphor for life,
for these straw-hatted men and women bending

to the clay. Remember Kavanagh,
who couldn't think his mother buried in that
Monaghan graveyard but was always with him

walking along a headland of green oats
in June? These workers toil beside their elders
always with them too, reminding them

that the earth is God, or near as makes no difference,
and each of us allowed a moment only,
one quick glimpse before we're sped away.

Oh Come All Ye
Trueborn Irishmen

*In memory of a young man murdered
by paramilitaries in 1975*

How to tell my feelings
when I think the way
they took you out and killed you,
dumped your body and
told no one where? Oh how

to tell my feelings when
I think your family
spent days and nights and months
and years believing, despite
everything, you'd turn up?—

That maybe you were warned
to leave and not come back.
Or maybe that they gave you
such a hiding or
disfigured you some way

that you were too ashamed
to show yourself at home
before the bruises and
the shame had faded, but
you would someday. You would,

someday — And that's the way
we keep on going, hoping,
praying. And all the time
they knew you were decaying
in that bog at Emyvale

and never said a word.
They could have said a word.
They could have said. Oh how
to tell my feelings when
I picture you tied up

and beaten, taken out
where no one goes (but only
they, for that) and told
to kneel and pray?— I can't
put words to things I see,

imaginings of you,
kneeling, like the way
the Nazis ordered Jews
to kneel on railway platforms
with necks bent forwards. Was there

a moment when you pleaded,
boy of seventeen—
your voice just broken out
of childhood, unbelieving
they will do this?— I feel

empty as the barrel
of the gun that fired
the bullet— Shattered as
the skull it cracked, the brain
it shredded. Lodged inside

my head these years that bullet.
Now they're digging up
those other people but
there's still no trace of you,
no bone, no leathered sinew,

not the slightest trace—
despite the messages
received anonymously,
with apologies for all
the hurt and suffering caused—

How to tell my feelings
when I read about
'apologies for all
the hurt and suffering caused'?
Oh, come all ye true-born

Irishmen and listen
to my song. Oh, tell me
where the Shelmaleers
that sunk you in the bog
are gone? Oh, did they die

for Ireland, or did any
one of them become
a Tollund Man to lie
unearthed 'till Old Ireland,
dear Old Ireland, might be free?

Street Demonstration Buenos Aires

This the city tourists come
to see the Tango demonstrations
in the streets. We're out already
early but everywhere armed police,
and here's the army band marching
to the Plaza de Mayo.

Full military regalia
makes terrific photographs —
but here's a ragged group behind,
a straggle of men and women shouting,
waving placards, something about —
THE MOTHERS OF THE DISAPPEARED...

Azucena Villaflor de De Vincenti.
Esther Ballestrino de Careaga.
Maria Ponce de Bianco...

the ones who sought the truth, their bodies
found in unmarked graves this week,
where they had lain for years, dragged out
from their home and family
the night before Our Lady's Feast Day,
nineteen hundred and seventy seven.

Death the price of searching out
the truth, the fate of those who VANISHED
WITHOUT TRACE... the husbands, brothers,
sons they'd lost and swore they'd find,
whatever was the cost. As always
in these matters, the cost was great.

Azucena Villaflor de De Vincenti.
Esther Ballestrino de Careaga.
Maria Ponce de Bianco...

Hard to follow a military band
all epaulettes and braid dressed up
to please the tourists. Hard not to tremble
at the sight of armed police
that lurk in corners, adjusting helmets,
tapping truncheons on their shields—

But they stumble on, their faces
set, their placards picturing
THE VANISHED WITHOUT TRACE — Convinced
that no remote abandoned shed,
or deep ravine or bog can hide
its plastic bags of bits forever...

Azucena Villaflor de De Vincenti.
Esther Ballestrino de Careaga.
Maria Ponce de Bianco.

Requiescat in pace.

PART III

". . . brief dalliance in the delicate garden of sweet poesy".

Where Do you Find Poetry?

The Bookstalls at Stazione Termini, Rome

(for Arcidio Baldani, poet, dates unknown)

Down the road from Termini the bookstalls
and their ancient owners husband out
their days - Such piles of old forgotten classics,
mounds of dog-eared fascist magazines -
such endless mouldering stacks of sad remainders
of that literary past where poets
thought that poetry could save the world,
then suffered through two wars that proved them wrong.

This man has spread his paper on a batch
of yellowed war-reports. This women smokes
among her pornographic videos.
And here a stall stands unattended
while its owner steps across the road
for coffee - But a friend has sidled in
behind the bargain Petrarchs and Pascolis
in case I might intend to make a purchase.

Dieci mila buys the 'Poesie'
of Arcidio Baldani, (nineteen
seventy five) - the tenth of the three hundred
autographed, with letters of reply
from notables, including Perugia's bishop
thanking but declining comment since
he is but churchman and not critic - but
is pleased to find the poems 'ampi', 'profondi'.

Where are you, my mirror image, now,
Arcidio? (Although I haven't fallen
to such letters, yet). A gravestone? Or
just old in some apartment block with cat
and kettle and long shelves of books
you'll never read again? I never met you,
but I think I know you well. Your verses
yearn for permanence, (that charlatan)

in face of flux (that tyrant). Must you close
your window to the disinfectant
that the city fathers nightly spray
in quantities as vast as that ambition
Mussolini showed your generation
with his chin? - His speeches heaped in piles
here in these bookstalls and as unread
as our poems, Arcidio. And look! -

Here under tourist guides and atlases
an old anthology in bad repair
but housing all the greats: Montale, Saba -
House we called on often, you and I,
unstoppable our urge to recreate
the world in words! I'm calling still, still browsing
in the bookstalls, sitting out the evening
into night. And sometimes writing something
like these lines for you, Arcidio. No. For us.

So Where Do You Expect to Find Poetry?

In yourself? — Where else? You write it out,
it seems just great. You type it out it seems
just crap. But yet, it's there, somewhere, in all
the bric a brac collected into corners,
words or phrases caught and stored in moments
when you didn't do the thing you should have—
Or did the thing you shouldn't have. The line
was taut, the strain was promising — You stood
your ground but then the snap, the glimpse of silver
vanishing downstream, the rod grown slack...

So where do you expect to find poetry?

In a newspaper? No. And Yes.
Sometimes there is a poetry box stuck up
the corner of the page to hold the words
in case they might escape, disturb the walls
of prose outside, which at that very moment
gets to grips with the serious issues and problems
of our society: who's divorcing whom,
what Bono has for his tea, and whether or not
What'shername will win the Kerry by-election —
No piddling around with fancy imagery and how
we might as humans be congenitally inclined
to kill our neighbours, kill the planet, kill
ourselves — That's poetry! This is prose. The stuff
that tells it straight. The real world of prose
to which the reader will return when his
(or her or its) brief dalliance
in the delicate garden of sweet poesy
(i.e., here in the poetry box) has ended.
Well, Lee Jaffe* proved that 30 seconds
is the max that most us will stick
with 'art', not least amid the mothball smell
of words that don't immediately make sense
and lines that arbitrarily end and never
make it to the margins. That's enough
of that for now. Let's see the crossword...

So, where do you expect to find poetry?

In a poetry book? — The auguries are good:
The lines don't reach the margin's edge, (see
above) the headings are obscure, there is
a definite lack of sense, and everything
is very personal. Must be poetry. And
furthermore the book is put together
by a bunch of poets, and they must know
what poetry is?— If they're any good
as poets, and they must be if they're in
the book? And sure enough they've put in lots
and lots of their own stuff, with grainy photos
of themselves in that familiar pose
in which they face the camera punching themselves
or holding their faces up with their hands while wearing
all the while withal that poets' smile
that gives you to understand the muse is near.
So do not fear: these are guaranteed
to be the top-notch poems the cover says
they are. These are the professionals
after all. You know you're not being had,
not being the victim of a sly attempt
to steal your feelings while your intelligence
isn't looking. But look at the price! Hang on.
Might pick it up later on, second hand...

So where do you expect to find poetry?

At a poetry reading? — Well, it's a poetry reading.
And with live poets who declaim
in that communicative monotone
aka The. Poetry. Voice.
That. Tries. To. Invest. Words.
With. An. Impor. Tance. They.
Would. Not. Possess, if you spoke them in
an ordinary way like this, you know what I mean?
And as a bonus at no extra cost
you're treated to some very long, some very
convoluted introductions three
and four and several times again the length
of the poem itself, along with all the usual
personal and ultimately unchallengeable
(and therefore unverifiable) explanations,
qualifications, justifications. Definitely
poets. But so high your expectations,
so verily convinced are you that poems
will be found here at this Poetry Reading
roaming unfenced fields at will, instead of

being corralled in the 'Poet's Corner' (see
above) under the picture of the Quill
or the usual baldy graphic of the Bard
in Ruff and Whiskers - Oh so very full
are you of expectation that you feel
somehow a disappointment and a shame
to see these poor bedraggled creatures
of the broken line reach out to you
from underneath enormous smothering mounds
of personal baggage, crying to be heard,
desiring that their incoherent pain
will be remembered. Only thing: this chair
is very hard and there's a draught behind me...

So, where do you expect to find poetry?

At the Open Mic? — Okay, but first
you have to find the Open Mic, that
transmigration of unquiet souls
doomed to roam from pub to pub forever,
chanting their interminable verse. The bouncer
at the International tells you, no
I haven't seen them in months. Some kind of row?
And then the barman down at Slattery's says
not since before the room was needed for
the lap dancers and that was weeks ago
but thinks they might be down in Brogan's,
you'd never know. But Brogan's scratches its head —
Try the Duke. And after that you try out
several gay bars on the offchance
that what the general public think of poets
might be true. But no. It seems that, mostly,
poets are closet heterosexuals. Don't
give up: eventually you'll run them to ground
in some back room or basement slated for change
of ownership or renovation or
demolition and there they are — Young poets
with not much of a clue but trying to work
towards something that might be poetry some day
in the far distant future. And old poets,
much wiser, experienced, and full of years
with not much of a clue but trying to work
towards something that might be poetry some day
in the far distant future. And you sit there
and listen to some guy eating the mic
and going on and on about where do you
expect to find poetry? Well, here,

dickhead. And if you have to write about
the writing about the poetry then you must have
nothing to write about. Still, good stuff —
A lot of it much better than your stuff,
and for once these people seem to care
about the audience and whether or not
they're listening or dropping off to sleep—
Well, that's a change! But is it poetry?
On the late bus home a cola-can
is rattling across the aisle. You stop it, ask it
tell me this, O cola-can, does such
a thing as poetry exist? The can
escapes. 'Maybe it does,' it shouts, crashing
down the stairs, 'But maybe again it doesn't'.
Infinite the wisdom of inanimates...

So, where do you expect to find poetry?

In your kitchen?— Well, okay. You're in
the kitchen, place where Life confronts us daily
with straight questions, and you're filling up
the dishwasher and you're listening to the news
and you hear a woman telling how
she had to leave her village, take her children
and whatever chattels she could carry
over mountainous terrain because
they came in trucks the night before and took
her husband and the other men away
but not away enough she couldn't hear
the shooting in the fields. And all through this
her voice is calm, her broken English slow,
her sorrow held back, trembling in her words
the way you'd hold an injured bird and yes,
you think, this is the rod that bears the pull
and strain of what is indescribable,
of what is unimaginable. And no,
you never thought to find it here beside
the football and the weather report and whether
or not What'sisname will run again
for re-election. And you lay aside
the sweeping brush and dust-pan, sit and listen
to her words that never saw the page,
her words demanding they be written. And
you know you'll have to write them, though you know
she'll never read them — Maybe no one will.
And even if you only catch the gaps
between her words it might be poetry.

The Fugitive Muse

For Tommy Halferty

You say it was the daily rape
drove you from my classroom. Stunned,
I watched you rouge your cheeks, put on
mascara, run your tongue on lipstick,

take a taxi into town. How
terrible those endless days
of searching out the places where
you'd most least likely be (you see

how well I know you, dear). At last,
the six-foot lesbian who holds
Fitzwilliam Square demurred at first,
then sold you back to me - So pale

and drawn and unforgiving. Better
far (you snarled) be whore dark wintry
nights near Leeson Bridge than fingered
for five years, then Publicly

Examined, poked and probed, pubic
juices oozing onto desk-tops,
a kind of fossilised graffiti...
See, my dear, my tears to see you

stand in lamplight at the kerb
determined to waylay each cruising
car - What quatrains have passed hands
across those lowered windows? For

that extra fiver will you offer
that so often you denied
to me? - That sudden burst of clear
translucent verse... No, no! Stay where

you are. We'll have another coffee
here in the Pembroke Bar. We'll
renegotiate our terms
of endearment, you and I -

I plead - I beg you will return.
I promise no more sacrifice
to inky adolescence – Tenderly,
I'll weigh each smallest hyphen

would best fit the narrow slit
between two syllables, then cover
you with careful kisses, love,
that you will stay with me forever.

We're Talking Poetry, Right?

Homage to Charles Bukowski 1920-1994

Wrestling with The English Language, trying
to land a foot on some flat patch of ground,
travelling the universe with Holst beside me
(angry Mars, ethereal Venus) and.
Bukowski. Orbiting my head with stuff
not lifted up and stacked way out of reach
with *French quotations*. Not stuff stored away
in leather-bound editions waiting for
the day it will be in demand. That is
to say (we're talking poetry, right?) never.

Nor was he ever lover of Latinate
constructions like: *nor was he ever lover*.
Neither did he try to rescue words
were hurtling towards obscurity. For him,
redundant particles long sheered off
the mother planet were best left to fling
themselves around some Saturnalean scrap heap—
Him, he wanted talk you'd hear in diners
or what passes for a conversation
at the racetrack when the ponies don't perform.

And yes for sure he drank too much (especially
in his poetry). And, sure. He had
Dark Moments (we're talking poetry, right?).
But when the chips were down (like, every week)
and when his room was full of empty bottles
(every night) he still could see through all
his glasses clearly... There's Jupiter now! Those chords.
The Giant — A ball of gas, it's said. It's said
that if you got to land on him you couldn't
stand on him (we're talking poetry, right?)

You're out there somewhere, Charles, with Holst — Maybe
you're standing with him in the Big Red Spot
conversing on the multitudinous tortures
mortals must endure for being human
(you're talking poetry, right?) and How One Might
Alleviate Them with hard liquor, women,
cigarettes, a horse or two a week
to come up trumps, a battered typewriter
and — who would think to find this on the list?! —
Poetry. Yes. We're talking poetry. Right!

The Dogs in the Street and Divers Other Mongrel Cliches, D'ye Know Whar I Mean, Like?

The dogs in the street knew well that the politicians were gettin'
big brown envelopes from the land developers
and they knew those envelopes weren't given for nothin',
d'ye know whar I mean, like? It's common knowledge too the dogs
in the street all knew that gun-crime would take off like a rockah
once the criminals got themselves organised. And the dogs
in the street knew that once the scares about the penalty points
wore off we'd start to slaughter ourselves on the roads again
like there was no tomorrah, d'ye know whar I mean, like?
An Airedale I knew a while back once told me he knew for a fact,
and even before it was a fact, that Conor Murphy should have
lined out for Galway last year — Selectors my arse, he said,
they don't know nothin'. D'ye know whar I mean, like? And I met
with a greyhound last year sleeps rough in a laneway off Dame Street
turned out to be top-informed about the shortage of beds
in our hospitals long before it became really bad — But
d'ye think that anyone would listen to *him*? — Nor at all. At the end
of the day, he's only a dog in the street, that's all, they said.
And what does a dog in the street know about hospitals? Nothin'. —
Although accordin' to what you hear on the radio, and read in the papers
and see on TV, the dogs in the street are supposed to know everything,
d'ye know whar I mean like?— My own dog, Elvis, though stric'ly speakin'
not a dog in the street — He's got a home, right? Anyways,
Elvis is out there a lot, keepin' his nose to the ground,
and his ear to the door, and his eye on the ball and he often hears things
you wouldn't believe, d'ye know whar I mean, like? Un-
be-lieve-able. That property bubble, for instance that nobody
thought would ever explode— Now everyone says that even
the dogs in the street knew it couldn't continue. Even
the dogs in the street. Me, I've never said the Irish
are the most intelligent nation on earth, the sharpest tools
in the toolbox, or the brightest bulbs on the Christmas tree.
No. Nor at all. Bur, at the end of the day it has to be said,
and there's no getting' 'round it, there's no two ways abour it — We do have
the most intelligent dogs in the street. D'ye know whar I mean, like?

On the West Lake, Hangzhou, China —
Where Poetry is Gained in Translation

At Hangzhou's West Lake, the mountains brood
in several shades of blue, the lake itself
encompasses an endless churn of greens
and greys and English is embroidered into
something other than itself by the tongue
was fashioned under Qin, and Han, and Song —
All ill-content until its foreign cousin
wear its robes, allow its folds to settle,
find an unexpected colouring shimmer
out through factual Anglo-Saxon vowels.

"First we see the island of 'Three Pools
Mirroring The Moon'". Our pleasure boat
moves from the harbour and the tour guide
points ahead. "So-called, because the people
come here for the Festival of the Moon
when she is full and she is recreated
in the waters. Then 'Mid-Lake Pavilion',
and to the left you see the island we call
'Ruan's Mound Encircled By Blueness', then
'The Orioles Singing In Ripples Of Willows'".

As the boat cuts gently through the waters,
and we sail towards 'Lotus Swaying In The Breeze'
and 'Misty Trees By The Nine Bend Stream'
her naming of these places springs a latch,
and once again I'm in the schoolroom chanting
litanies of the pure and beautiful —
"Vessel of Honour, Singular Vessel of Devotion,
Mystical Rose, Tower of David, Tower
of Ivory, House of Gold, Ark of the Covenant,
Gate of Heaven, Morning Star..."

'Autumn Moon Over The Calm Lake',
'Leifing Pagoda Standing In The Sunset',
'Melting Snow Hanging Over Broken Bridge',
'Viewing Fish In The Flowering Harbour', 'Greenness
Spouting From The Yellow Dragon's Mouth', 'To Dream
Of The Tiger-Pawing Spring', 'Two Peaks
Piercing The Sky', 'Night Bell Tolling
Against The Southern Bank', 'Spring Dawn
Around The Su Causeway', 'Cloud Flying
Over The Jade Emperor's Hill...'.

The language wrought by Zhou and Tang and Ming
prefers, like West Lake's brooding mountains
several shades of bluenesses fading
into grey, and like the West Lake's waters,
it inclines towards endless interminglings
of dark greens and off-white plumes of spray
and poetry is what is gained in the translation —
Those 'Orioles Singing in Ripples of Willows',
those 'Misty Trees by the Nine Bend Stream',
and Oh! Those 'Two Peaks Piercing the Sky!'

Do Not Impede Enjambment
While the Poem is in Motion

Like every railway timetable will list
within its times and schedules possible routes
for all, a poem has seats to spare (and more)
for those will climb aboard. Stand up and clutch
the handle of your hold-all on the page's
edge — There's something in the way the stanzas

hurtle towards you. Yes! Towards insignificant
you! The man in cap and braid will check
your ticket and demand the reason for your fears.
Choke back your tears and answer honestly,
allow the poem to tremble, shunt and creak
and gather speed past stations you missed out

before and others closed you thought might still
be open. And you find the stanzas filled
with strangers, and the few you used to know
now turn their faces to the window. No
excuses now. No lies or half-truths here.
You must endure these silver lines that rush

along together, lifting you past nettled
sidings breaking off towards nowhere (once,
once there was a time, a chance...). You mourn
the long-abandoned buildings, grieve the wreckage
of old transports, weep for each enjambment
of the gleaming blades that cut past every junction,

whip past every nameplate, blurring faces,
figures, someone waving, some who stand
unmoving (you know why) until you sense
a slowing down, a hiss, a final shudder,
emptiness. And that familiar shade
that's followed you a lifetime? Yes he's there

and beckoning you descend. Now gather up
your bowl and coin and smile, be glad to be arrived
at this last stanza, hear your footsteps crunch
the gravel, hear the turnstile whine. Do not
regret the way poem has clanked itself together,
blows a whistle, and begins to move away.

Too Much Talk About the Muse

Too much talk about 'the Muse' when talking
poetry and difficulties thereof.
Too much thinking that, besides the poets,
anyone anywhere really gives a toss.

The time has come, therefore, to see off Milton.
And his 'Sisters of the Sacred Well'.
Forget the classic 'invocations', tell
the truth: a poem is like an aching tooth,

and nothing more. A vague uneasiness
that stabs the root of memory, sets up
a constant phrase that throbs long into night
 when sleep fails and the driving rain

interrogates the window and it seems
like day will never break again. And were it
just a tooth, it could be pulled. But root
of poetry? How? - And so next morning down

to Milton's surgery, reclining chair.
'I knew you would be back' he says. His muse
(in white, beside him) hands him torch and probe.
'I've tried out various forms,' I stammer. 'Thought

if I broke free from scansion, stanza, verse -
you know, all that old-hat Olympian style...'
The muse and Milton smile indulgently.
'They all say that,' he laughs. 'Now, open wide...'

How to Succeed at Poetry
and Make a Lot of Yen
(As seen on TV!!!)

Saw this Japanese lady on TV
talking about her life, her feelings, and
her relationships and how she uses
her computer programme to write poetry
about them. First, she clicks the drop-down box,
then picks the Tanka (that strict form as used
by Japanese poet-scribes since ancient times),
its lengths and lines. And then she adds her life,
her feelings, and her relationships and out
the other end comes poetry. And, before
you start to snigger, I must tell you that
this lady is quite famous in Japan,
has three best-sellers and makes a lot of Yen.

So much for my best efforts year on year
(since ancient times) to tie up Pegasus
in my back garden, muck his stable out
and clean his leavings into organised heaps.
It's time I got me one of them there
Japanese Tanka computer programmes, fed it into
my C Drive, and then typed in my life,
my feelings, and my relationships, and then
sat back and watched it fire out poetry
about three times as quick as shit from a shovel
and never mind the quality, feel the width.
And if it looks like poetry it must
be poetry. Especially if you end up
on the TV *(omigod!)*. Especially
if it's all about your life, your feelings
and your relationships. Especially if
it's written as a Tanka *(he's so clever!)*.
And especially if you make a lot of Yen.

OMIGOD, Not Another Newgrange Poem

with some indications as to delivery 'a la mode'

(Please strike a pose consonant with
the dignity of the lines you are about to deliver)
It is an ancient law enacted by
Aosdána that every Irish Poet be moved
to write about Newgrange once every year
for competitions, or to be declaimed
to multitudes in a monotonous poetry voice
(like this) while standing in the pouring rain

beside the ruins. Said poets should write, nay, sing
about the silence of her ancient stones,
the roundness of her ancient stones, the hardness
of her ancient stones, the ancientness
of her ancient stones, the stoniness of her ancient
stones. And how it is they yearly speak
to us *(No, no! Read that again, and this time*
lift the voice on 'us') … And how they yearly

speak to *us* across millenniums, nay,
millennia *(Pause. Significant pause,*
look up, stare at the audience, look down. Sigh).
And how the solstice penetrates her passage
yearly on the front page of 'The Irish Times'.
And how the nation yearly feels the need
to re-discover prehistoric roots.
Or prehistoric Truths. Or. Booth.

And how the Nation casts its gaze back
to those ancient days *(more feeling!)* …
to those ancient days when men were men
and ate their meat raw, sucked the bones,
and dressed in off-the-shoulder furs, went clubbing
for their women, and had a deep relation-
ship with stones and knew the stars and how
to roll enormous rocks on poles (small 'p')

up from the Boyne Valley. Knew to carve
involved and complicated rings and loops
with their ancient tools, and knew the Mystery
of Life Itself, *(pause)* and how to chart
the sun *(look up and pause again)* to make it
strike along this passageway. Today
it can be done at any-old-tourist-time
thanks to the Board of Works installed a light

to creep along the floor when it's switched on
like this: (*!) Excuse me, sir, but could you move
your foot a little... Thank you. (Bloody tourists!)
Now behold! *(step back and gesture towards
the floor)* The Sacred Light that lit the dark
before old Moses was a boy in britches!
See *(step back again and mind your head)*
The Sacred, Sacred Light that every year

attracts ten thousand weighty poems, replete
with abstruse references to the Druids, each poem
ten thousand times the weight, and more, of Newgrange,
and all her ancient stones. (*!)... Mind your heads
on the way out and please don't help yourselves
to free souvenirs. It costs a fortune to replace
these old stones with new ones every year.
And there's a bucket for tips at the entrance. Don't fall over it.

His Despairing Friends

Everyone pities the poet. He's a bit daft
in the head. Given to thinking on things a bit
too much and mooning around in the mornings, tackling
the distance between the kettle and teapot like
you'd set out to cross the Atlantic on a homemade raft,
or set up to check out the insides of the Titanic
with a waterproof suit and a torch and one of them fancy
robot cameras. But, no use complaining,
we have to put up with him because of the way he combs
through the mountains of rubbish we talk ourselves through
                                         every day —

It's a dirty job, but poets have to do it.
They're like those shantytown kids that live on the dollar
they get for the metals and bottles they pick from the dumps
on the edge of the city, and sometimes come up clutching
something that might be, might be, valuable — Hey!
We thought we 'd lost that! Well, whaddayaknow! —

But this, just very occasionally. It's mostly
having to sit forever on creaky chairs
extremely hard on the arse and listen to him
pontificating down on top of us in verse
until we begin to ask ourselves how come
we're here, listening to desperate poets when
we could be at home watching 'Desperate Housewives' or
'I'm a Celebrity, Get Me Out of Here!' —
What time is it? Dear Lord, hear my prayer:
Get me out of here before death claims me!
Still, as I said, it's no use complaining, he
is our friend. And it's good to see him above with the mike
in his hand, doing the thing he does best and no one
does better— Talking shite and making a prick
of himself. But that's okay. Thanks be to God
for the poets, I say. It could've been me up there.

Especially When

Especially when the day has worn you down
is when to write it, even while the moth
is circling the light and all your millstones
hang around you and your gravestones weigh
your heart is when to write it. Even if
it feels your hands are severed at the wrist,
your eyelids sliced (and it's been done) is when
to write the thing has been about to spring
across the synapse rods all day but then
stayed hovering. Some bait was needed. Maybe
a copse of trees? Or a locked door? Maybe
a car park where the weeds and nettles threatened
through the rusting fence? Or flash of sunlight
from an opening window? But the moment
slipped and now these minutes just before
the shutter falls it will be hard. But then
there's never an especially when. It's always.

How Oft in Spirit Have I Turned to Thee

Oh cruel King of Darknesses, imploring
that you deal with those who dealt me grief
and grant them warm hospitality
in your Stygian depths in the next world:—
Those visitors to my house who brought my children

sticky lollipops that stuck to cushions,
carpets, curtains— Satan, I entreat you
to prepare your roasting spits for them,
and leave some space for all the chewing gummers
who destroyed the arse of many a good trousers.

Remember too those 'friends' who rubbished books
I lent them— 'Don't know what you saw in that'—
But then neglected to return them:
"Oh, I passed that on to John. I didn't think
you'd mind". A five-pronged fork for these, please.

And I implore you, Nick, to stick a few more
faggots on the fire for the *'wroiters'* who thought
their convoluted nonsense would improve
if they stuck in some 'fucks' and 'cunts'.
It didn't. Oh, Beelzebub, bring out

your boiling cauldrons for those family members
(No. No mercy here) who commandeered
the remote control entire evenings, flicking
flicking, flicking: "Who'd pay a licence fee
to watch this crap?"— Did someone mention my wallet?

And what about the *can-can canna-*
canna can can canna behind me
on the bus?— "Hi sweety!" Then the long,
excruciatingly intimate conversation...
May the Dark One fry their earlobes...

A list like this might never end (such was
my tortured life) but I reserve to last
the *fiends* I hated most: the poets who wrote
shite that got published, while great stuff like this
never got a look-in. Lucifer, don't fail me.

Song of the Wandering Suburbanite

"I went out to the hazel wood
because a fire was in my head..." W.B. Yeats

I take the bus to town to find myself. And
here I am in the Central Library
where silent men read papers all day long:
Will any heart now laugh at my emotion?

The Poundstores peddle clothespegs, plasticcrap
and corn plasters - crowded to the doors
with busy housewives bargainhunting: Which
of you today would be my mistress? Muse?

The pigeons piss on Dan O'Connell's head
and young backpackers eye him, tick their lists.
Please, take me with you back to Austria,
or Greece or Dwight (Kentucky). Anywhere

will do: the poorest crofter's hut in Scotland,
equally St Mark's expensive fraud,
or Greenland of the geyser-heated streets—
Whatever clime the sun's bright circle crawls.

Eason's magazines: I read through one
or two until I'm asked politely please
do not. She's very nice of course. Of course
she doesn't know I've had a poem in Cyphers.

Tea, and watch Kingburger change the guard
and think: how easier navigate the pillars
breached by Hercules than pay the mortgage
yearly, see the balance scarcely change.

I buy a dog-eared Keats and sit up top
and whisper to the bus: You've saved my life again.
They go insane who only stand and wait
for silence from the lawnmowers of suburbia.

Time Will Come There's Nothing Left

In memory of Ted McNulty d.1998

Time will come there's nothing left
of hand. Not field, flower nor woman
have the power to break the white
that blinds the heart. Unknown the when
will come that furious final act
of putting down the pen forever,

pen that waits in folded dark
the hand will take it out from coins,
receipts, bus tickets, bric-a-brac
of life's untidy edges, waits
for hand will draw it out for shop-list,
crossword puzzle, milkman's note

and - when the blood sings - tap temple,
ease along the lip, submit
to tongue until a line of figures
break the white where nothing was
before. And time will come his jacket,
shrugged into his shape and stoop,

will hang for weeks until it settle
out of him, its pockets emptied,
one or two things set aside
as useful: key, some coins, the pen
that stands an idle month, a year,
a time until it shed his touch,

his slanting it to page, becomes
again 'pen', fit for any hand
would take it, break the blinding white
because the time will come there's nothing
left of hand but never time
will come there's nothing left to write.

PART IV

"liturgies and broken monologues, a sigh, a sob..."

Pinturicchio: Saint Agostino and the Child Who Wishes to Empty the Sea

Bernardino di Betto, detto il Pintoricchio, 'Pala di Santa Maria dei Fossi': predella: (dettaglio) sant'Agostino e il bambino che vuole svuotare il mare. Galleria Nazionale, Umbria. (Soprintendenza Beni Storici Artistici ed Etnoantropologici dell'Umbria - Perugia (Italy).

TVIVF

Anyone seen that TV clip they show
when In Vitro Fertilisation is in the news?
There's this bunch of spermatozoids playing around
like schoolyard urchins and thrashing their tails and not
doing harm to anyone, and least of all to that
enormous big blob thing to the left of your screen —
that's the egg — and then from out of nowhere
comes this pointy tweezers thing and snatches
one of the sperm chaps who's been hanging around
on the edge of his group and whisks him up and away
from his pals and shoves him into the egg. I believe
God gave us the remote control for moments like this.

I look at the news to keep me up to speed
on things like road deaths, gangland murders, tortures,
sexual perversions in religious institutions— These
things I can handle. They're part of the way we are.
But this is different. Nothing natural about
the way those tweezers grab the sperm and squeeze it
to make it fit, just as much as to say:
"Enough with the swishing around in the gravy, laddie!
Or did you think that all this procreation
paraphernalia was invented just
for fun? — Get in there and get a life!"
Omigod! It gives me such a pain in the crotch to watch it.

Towards an Understanding
of People who Talk to Themselves
on the Public Thoroughfares

They have great regrets, these people who talk
to themselves on the public thoroughfares, communing
with their dead - to whom no recompense
or just atonement now is possible
for wrongs inflicted when the tides were high.

Living enemies surround them too,
so hence their re-enactment of the sharp
retort they should have thought of at the time,
instead of moments afterwards, on the stairway,
argument lost, the heart a raging torrent.

Heads bowed in the presence of their ghosts,
they will address the pavements, stand in silence
in the traffic isles or at the kerbside
while the lights change and the passers-by
decide to step around them. They could shout

aloud above the surge of cars and buses
but instead they murmur liturgies,
and broken monologues, a sigh, a sob
betokening the absence of a son,
a wife, from whom too much was asked, too long.

Come evening, they will stand behind the curtain,
watch the streetlamps flicker up and turn
to find the room is peopled out again
with shadows, mute, but waiting for the word
was left unsaid, the act that could have stanched

the wound, the thing could have been done that moment,
moment now so distant, moment now
so many tens of years ago, an island
several seas away, where — could we but beach
again its shoreline — everything might be changed.

An Old Man Makes Love

The dog strains at the leash, his nose
flat up against the plate-glass. Still
his master hesitates ('Down, sir,
I say! Down, boy!'). Behind her,
paperback romances bulge
and magazines sell thighs and sloping
towards her breasts are every kind
of sweet the mouth could water for.

She laughs and hears a music fill
her laughter, feels her silver chain
ride up around her throat and knows
this old man pays his court to her
and her alone each morning here
on Mobhi Road where buses pass
and passers-by are courtiers
a moment only. Hat and stick

his only helmet, sword — and she
his Guinevere in skirt and blouse.
And he a knight so modestly
uncertain how to broach his love.
And she, unschooled in courtly ways,
embarrassed to receive, surprised
to see his stoop and muddled look
abruptly cast aside, to hear him

fashion out a language full
of high desires and coy deceits
so flattering she must return
this lovers' litany of naming:
he's 'a wicked man', a 'rogue'
and she 'a pearl', a 'gem', and how
those lips devour his heart, and how
those painted nails peel off the years,

that neck, those shoulders - Mad with love
he takes the cigarettes and paper,
thrusts his hand in hers a moment,
feels their bloods run parallel
an instant, then begins the slow
withdrawal and still the dog whines,
customers push past and he
must fall away, become again

an old man out on Mobhi Road
where buses pass and passers-by
are courtiers a moment only,
dog intent on nosing out
that bitch of yesterday ('Down,
sir, I say!'). At Cross Guns Bridge
he leans to see his head and shoulders
undulate below, his face
float smooth, unwrinkled on the waters.

IT'S THAT MAN AGAIN!!!

And at last it's feet up in the evening,
now for a beer, a spot of TV, and—
don't I deserve it, after getting through
another daily dose of bullshit and bellyaching —
now for a bit of personal time, a bit
of ME-time, a splash of the goggle-box —
OH NO! It can't be! **IT'S THAT MAN AGAIN!!!**
Jesus Christ! — No, I don't mean 'Jesus Christ'.
I mean: Jesus Christ! **IT'S THAT MAN AGAIN!!!**
saluting, waving, embracing crowds — Just where
the hell would TV be without him?! Well,
the so-called 'History Channels' anyway,
and nothing much in the documentary slots
on all the rest but 'Anniversary Programmes'
they put on to make good goddamn sure

we don't let sleeping Japanese or Germans
lie for long in case they might forget
what evil, nasty buggers they were once
until WE straightened them out with Hiroshima
Nagasaki, Dresden. And never a night
allowed to pass but HE is wheeled out, and
especially when the television schedules
aren't tight, or when they're fresh out of fodder
for the gaping multitudes (of which,
yes, I am one). I'm sitting there, deciding
whether or not to take my socks off or
get up and fetch another can of beer and —
There he is! **IT'S THAT MAN AGAIN!!!**
IT'S HIM AGAIN! Addressing crowds again,
gesticulating, ranting, grimacing—

or being nice and playing with his dog.
And where the hell is the remote? — But no!
There's no escaping him! He's everywhere!
On BBC he's masterminding ruin
for everyone he doesn't deem quite 'kosher'.
On Channel 4 he's spreading out his maps.
On UTV — No use. He's out to flatten
Russia on a level with her steppes,
his *einsatzgruppen* singing lustily
the *Deutschland uber Alles*... Yet — And yet
it always ends the very same, though only
after endless frames of speckled footage
and the lengthy reminiscences
of gnarled faces telling how he could
be charming. Yes, it always ends the same,

81

in spite of all the crowds, the motorcades,
the sycophantic henchmen, all the hands
uplifted in that straight salute — It always
ends the same with that great aerial shot
of the Reichstag burning and I think (socks
off by now) thank God he's gone for one night.
Must be snooker on somewhere — Let's see
the TV Guide? — A spot of football, maybe?
Where's those Girls of Playboy Mansion? But
NO! It can't be! **IT'S THAT MAN AGAIN!!!** —
Jesus Christ! No! I don't mean 'Jesus Christ'.
I mean: Jesus Christ! **IT'S THAT MAN AGAIN!!!**
IT'S HIM!!! — But wait! It's only part of him!
They've found a bit of skull in a paper bag
on a shelf in some old dusty war-archive

somewhere in downtown central Moscow. And —
They've made a programme out of it, with lots
of that old footage seen a thousand times
before, plus coloured bits they've made themselves
stuck in to liven up the show. Cue
gnarled faces, same as seen before
(It's true! Old soldiers never die! Especially
those who talk in Russian with subtitles).
Then an expert in white coat comes on
and tells at length that if you open up
a box and find a bit of someone's head
you can be fairly sure they're fairly dead.
At last, I think. He's dead at last. And now,
that beer. And now those 'Desperate Housewives'. But ...
But no! Another sciency chap comes on

and starts to question whether or not that bit
of skull is part of THAT MAN'S skull. It might be.
Then again, it just might not... And now
I'm on my knees and pleading with the screen. —
Have mercy. Please let him be finished off.
Just for tonight?! One night! A single night
without the Reich was built to last ten million
television documentaries!
Relentlessly the sciency chap goes on
and on and on and then there's shots of labs
and microscopes and then the screen fills up
with stuff they say was never seen before
and then— **IT'S THAT MAN AGAIN!!!** Yes,
IT'S HIM AGAIN!!! The trench coat. Peaky hat.
The toothbrush 'tash. The staring eyes. I'm sorry,

I just can't go on...

Concerning an Excursion
Into the Rainforest

Yes, we went to see the monkeys. See them
'in their natural habitat'. And when
we clambered from the boat — such mud! such laughter!—
we were all in such high animal spirits.
especially me. I do love animals,
especially monkeys, though I'd never seen them
much, not close-up I mean, except
in pictures and in the zoo of course. I feel

there's very little separates us primates —
quite apart from brains, of course. And there's
a bit more DNA, I've heard. But then,
look where our brains have gotten us, homo
not-so-sapiens. Maybe we'd be
better off munching on bananas, swinging
tree to tree and all the sex you want
and when and where you want it. Anyway,

we're here on Monkey Island, squidging down
a winding trail of mud and vegetation —
such a lot of mud! such laughter! — and
our guides have gone ahead to find the monkeys —
Find the monkeys? Why? Are they hiding
from us? (Laughter) We're a merry bunch!
And then — a loud commotion, sounds of thrasings,
screamings, crashings — Monkeys scrambling out

before us, running, dodging, jumping, leaping
across our path, big males, youngsters, mothers
with their babies, faces angry, scared,
and so like us the way they yelp and grimace,
clamp their hands (or is it 'paws'?) across
their ears and still the guides are shouting, trashing
undergrowth. It's then I know how much
we make them suffer, these our near relations

on the evolutionary super-highway
bound for God knows (and only He knows) where
and we sure don't for all our brainpower. Truth is
every monkey knows as much as we
about the where we're headed. One thing, though,
they *do* know (and I know it now. I think
I knew it all along) is that they have
no welcome for us, coming here, rigged out

in rubber boots and raincoats, cameras at
the ready and our sensitivities set
to zero, to beat them from their homes to get
a better look at them close up, a better
picture to take back. They snarl and shout
(like you would too in their place) and definitely
I know they hate all this and hate us too
for doing it to them. And I feel ashamed.

The Martyrdom of St. Andrew

From the Affresco di Mattia Preti,
La Basilica di S. Andrea della Valle, Roma

These workmen pictured busy at their task
around the patient martyr must have wives
who will expect them home this evening, children
will expect a father's noisy greeting,
tiny gifts perhaps, yet here they strain
to tie the ankles down and reach to stretch
the arms and wrists and struggle to get purchase
for the ropes must hold him up for days.

In the church of Sant'Andrea della Valle
all is clear: all suffering and travail
become quite unremarkable to those
who have a job to do — The bombing team
above Baghdad concerned to minimise
the waste of ordnance — The orderly
who has to swab the walls in Buchenwald.
Or Preti's men who work with faces dark

with concentration but devoid of malice
towards this latest one the soldiers brought
this morning. And when death comes they will come
to take him down and take apart their cross
and leave him to his weeping relatives
(as angels unfurl banners overhead).
Evening sees them, elbows on the table,
telling with mouths full the news from town.

Tiler on a Rooftop Above Ujedz, Prague

Only a painter's stroke might best align
the angle of his stance when suddenly
he straightens, climbs so unconcernedly
along the naked lathes to fetch his hammer.
Sweep of brush might catch his careless arc
of backward reach before the hammer falls
to pin another slate - his body poised
against that fractional departure from
the mean would send him toppling downwards, that
same squaring up to nature Irish navvies

showed, astride the iron joists above
the New America they built - No harness,
helmet, just agility and skill
of living at the very edge of things
before old greybeard gravity drags all
down. The risks are great: unspeakable
the payment for a momentary stumble -
But the thrill of standing near to God!
Not being so grappled always to the earth!
And oh the chilling sweep of the Vltava!

St. Augustine and the Child

From the painting by Bernardino Pintoricchio (1454-1513)
in the National Gallery of Umbria, Perugia, depicting the saint
standing beside a child who kneels to empty the sea.

One morning centuries past he took a brush
and finished off this special plea: a child
with spoon and plate who stoops to undertake
a task so laughably impossible, and yet
whose haloed face betrays no doubts. Child
who kneels where waters neatly course to sea,
look how Augustine stands with hands upraised
and crozier slanted: How can you hope
to change the nature of the universe,
angelic child who kneels to empty the sea?

The morning bustles past this galleria
and fills Perugia's mediaeval streets
and we can count ourselves one sunrise older,
one noontide richer than the child today
become newsworthy - Broken child who lies
sprawled sideways on front pages, stomach
stitched with bullets, somewhere in the Gulf.
And death has such a way with innocence:
those half-closed eyes, that head turned slightly sideways
towards the camera, that half-open mouth...

Augustine smiles indulgently. Dissector
of the human soul, he's walked its deserts,
mapped its reefs and canyons. Now, this living
with each other... Those who seek out peace
must come armed only with humanity
and hope, must move against all grain of hate,
ignore all torrent, tide of spite, be like
this child that kneels beside vast waters,
work with spoon and plate determinedly
reclaiming dry land from the endless sea.

Is it Possible to be Elegant
On a Bicycle in Traffic in the Rain?

In Kyoto, yes: where bicycles are widely venerated,
cherished, loved, accoutred with the gloves that fit
around the handlebars, and springdown stands
that hold against all winds, and easily surmountable
low crossbars, wide soft-saddles, bells that ring
(discretely), baskets for your bread-rolls, paper,
early morning milk. No fancy paints, pretentious
water bottles, complicated gears or gadgets — See!
A Buddhist monk glides out the temple door,
unhurried, tranquil, coloured robes wound round
for safety, one hand to steer, the other to hold clear
his umbrella while he weaves through traffic,
his white socks and sandals snug in plastic overshoes
and safe against the rains that Brahma sent today.

So yes, it is quite possible to be elegant on a bicycle
in traffic in the rain and there's no strict requirement
one must worship at the temple shrine to learn to balance
handlebar, umbrella, inner peace and pedal against the rush
of cars and buses and the gaze of curious tourists. But
a little worship helps. And inner peace. And wide soft saddles.

Inanimates

The cup is waiting patiently. The kettle
bubbles towards the *click*. The shadows gather
slowly in their corners, while outside
the clothesline sways, the side-door swings, the fencing
sighs, the garden shed fades into dark.
   Unremarked the industry of inanimates.

The windowpane returns your stare — This night
the streetlamps light the thoroughfares in ways
you've never seen before because despite
the thousand times and more you've peered into
this street you've never seen this night before.
   Intricate the workings of inanimates.

The book is where you left it down (a page
has straightened upright overnight) beside
the glass of water standing still until
your footfall wakes a quiver. And the pencil
has remained long hours in readiness.
   Unsung the loyalty of inanimates.

Creation. Use / Display. And then destruction
or long years forgotten in the attic
until resurrection in the bootsale
or the antique shop, attaining to
another life of unperturbed existence.
   Extraordinary the resilience of inanimates.

Theirs, the peace that passes understanding.
Theirs, the span of life that will see out
the human biblical three score and ten.
And theirs, the state of silence and slow time
attained by Celtic broaches, Grecian urns.
   Zen the natural stasis of inanimates.

Homage to Maximilian Kolbe

b. Jan. 8th 1894 Zdunska Wola (Near Lodz) Poland
d. Aug. 15lh 1941 Auschwitz

That moment you stepped up to take his place
and let yourself be led down to the cells
below the death yard was the moment when
you stayed the pen of What or Who it is
writes up the pages of our reckoning.

The cells below the death yard: Block 11
where you and your nine companions starved,
the iron door each morning opened only
to drag out the dead and kick back those
who begged a piece of bread or drop of water.

But you made no requests, made no complaints,
gave courage to the rest as they grew weaker,
prayed with them in their last agonies.
Miraculously you lasted several days
so finally they took you out and killed you.

That moment that you offered them your life
for his what must have been their silence? Must
have been somewhere the noise of parchment tearing?
Who or What compiles our catalogue
of fierce and constant cruelties towards each other

must have covered several lengthy pages
in advance, given all the cold
and sharp predictabilities of evil.
But you spoke and forced whatever hand
or claw or cloven hoof it is endites

our sorry chronicles of hate to turn
another page and start afresh and write,
reluctantly, of Maximilian
and hope and how it came about that he
so loved his neighbour better than himself.

Teachers

Teachers talk and talk and smoke
at break time, confiscate
our cigarettes and lecture lecture
lecture us and all the time

we smell it off their clothes and breath
and hair (if they've any left).
Teachers wipe their glasses on their ties
(the female kind have always tissues

up their sleeves) and when they're asked
a question — just to pass the time —
they blow their noses, hum and haw, and
lecture lecture lecture us. Headcase

drives a rusty Ford, must open
bottles with those teeth, is always
late but when WE are gives out and says
he's in loco parentis, lectures us

and lectures us - He's loco alright.
Floozie's on the Board and God
but doesn't she half fancy her sweet self.
Big Meeting once a month: the famous

two piece navywhite, black tights
and shiny handbag. Joxer in his raincoat
at the bus stop trying not to see us
in our cars - My dad says it's no job

for a man. High-paid baby sitters,
my dad says. Hitler laughs a lot
on Fridays, spends weekends gardening.
Four different shirts, three ties and thinks

he knows something worth learning.

To the Memory of Edward Tenison, DD., and the Glorious Resurrection of His Church as a DIY/Decorating Centre Superstore This Poem is Dedicated

"The Church's Restoration
In eighteen-eighty-three
Has left for contemplation
Not what there used to be... "

From 'Hymn' by John Betjeman

To the memory of the Right Reverend Father in God
Edward Tenison DD, late Lord Bishop of Ossory,
departed this life November 29, 1735 AD,
in his 62nd year and whose plaque looks down
on the best ceramic tiles available in Dublin's city
centre: designs arrived just newly from Italy and Spain
in all good brands of quality (there's Kalebodur,
Kleine and Pilkington), this poem is dedicated.

Many a Sunday did the faithful decorate themselves
and sit in pews to parley with their Lord ~ Yea,
would they congregate to pray and deck the soul
in colours pleasing to Him, led by Edward Tenison,
His representative on earth. Yea, would they climb
their voices past the highest organ note, past
curtain rails and satins 60 inches wide, past
facingboard and every paint and stain and shade

the modern soul finds needful, nay, finds balm
to spirits pealed and stripped and sanded daily: Oh,
lift up your hearts and praise the wallpapers of suburbia
and walk with me in heaven, feast on tasteful decors,
double-glazing, sunken lighting, sliding door — These
hallowed boards he trod year after year now bend
beneath their rows of sealant, stacks of grouting pastes
and curious implements designed to paint a ceiling

without splashback, all his sermons stashed somewhere
that God has rented out to store such truck as time
has shelved for good. They were for Good. They were for God!
But even He, in His divine, unguarded moments
fain would cast them out (*His* mansions too could maybe do
with some refurbishment?). Fain would, but can't. (They're Edward's.
Edward Tenison's. One can't). So let poor churchmice gnaw
long into night until they break a tooth on texts

that dwell uncompromisingly upon the need
to sweep clean every crack and cleft and dusty shelf
and fling wide open every aperture will welcome
Grace of God. Remember, Edward, all those doubts
you had and nursed long winter nights beside your Ann
(beloved and commemorated here too) telling over
and again how it is said the Kingdom of the Good
will never fail, an we but rise each morning bent

upon remaking of ourselves. See, Edward, Heaven
come on earth around you: method, mean and mechanism
(all in handy packs) to smooth the rough, rebuild again
the fallen, stem the grim disintegration all
our masonry is heir to. Yea, verily I say:
the lion of solemn vespers here lies down beside the lamb
of pelmets, curtains and Swish-Rail. *Excuse me, Can you
help me? I want a can of outdoor paint. And, oh yes, a brush*

The Emperor Advises

I dreamed of you tonight, Marcus Aurelius,
wise emperor, I dreamed you draped
your purple cloak across a bush at evening,
pushed a tiny boat on lapping waters,
shipped the oars and beckoned me on board.

We sailed the seven seas quite unimpeded,
you and me, Marcus Aurelius, you patiently
explaining all the myriad forms on sea beds,
all of moving things incarnate, all
the sirens songs and on and on until
we landed safe again. I dreamed I stood

embraced by you, Marcus Aurelius, one moment
on the pebbled shore while winds stood still
and moorhens fell all silent. Then, you took
the purple cloak again and tucked your toes
in latticed sandals, smiled and pressed my hand

and said: This little boat is life itself—
We sail, we reach the shore, we disembark.
Remember while this mortal clay is trembling
towards the dark, be certain that you weigh
whatever rhetoric you choose. Remember
to be certain that you own the words you use.

Bosnian Housewife

(Visoko 1996. From a news photo)

"The world revolves like ancient women
Gathering fuel in vacant lots" - T.S. Eliot

She wears the loosely-waisted dress of women
who've borne children, become broad-hipped.
She slips her coloured headscarf off in that
well-practised twist of thumb on knot and holds it

close against her nose and mouth. Her hair,
clipped short, is windswept and she smoothes it
as she steps among the tables, slowly,
weighing up the best cuts off the bone,

the bits might make a soup, the scraps would feed
the dog. For months no supermarket shelf
has shown such wide display, but here today
her housewife's eye is clouded. Here today

on offer, crated, hosed of all the mud
they shared for months lie husbands, fathers, sons
of Visoko, each reassembled frame
of rib and rag to be identified

as what is left of a beloved. She
moves slowly past each figure, twisted rigid
in his last sharp foetal agony. She
scans the names and number tags. A skull

stares back, its mandible looped, respectfully,
along the box's edge. The man with clipboard
comes and whispers. Yes, she nods. Yes.
And a camera whirrs and she becomes

Niobe, yes, still as rock, but tearless.
Yes, she's Deianeira too, but yet
won't kill herself for love but carry this
last Yes for all that's left of all her days

and nights. She signs. Yes. And collects
his keys and coins, steps into cratered streets,
becomes again a housewife scouring shops
for milk, fresh vegetables, a little meat.

Annunciations on a Journey
Through the Outskirts of Milan

"L 'angel che venne in terra col decreto
de la molt'anni lagrimata pace,
ch'aperse il cielo del suo lungo

divieto,dinanzi a noi pareva si' verace
quivi intagliato in atto soave,
che non sembiava imagine che tace."
— Dante, 'La Divina Commedia', Pugatorio X, 34-39.

"The angel that came to earth with the edict / of that many-years tearfully-awaited
peace / that opened Heaven from long interdict / before our eyes appeared so
truly / carved here in gracious act /that he seemed not a silent image." (Author's
translation)

Life undisguised, enunciating windows
wedged with cardboard, clotheslines waving shirts,
houseplants bursting out of fractured pots,
and wildflowers overwhelming rusting cars
that squint their headlamps blind-eyed at the sun
like old men watching shadows lengthen out
across the stones of their piazza, waiting
for that final hour, that thieving hand
will take them, all their days become
as wrapped in memories as we are trapped
in sleepy morning haze of travellers
journeying through the outskirts of Milan.

What splendid angel of the Lord descend
into this landscape? Where is she would stand,
head bowed before a Leonardo-crafted
Gabriel would come with whirr of wing
and radiant face to proffer flower and call her
blessed? Could it be that signorina
sipping coffee on her balcony
(who barely turns her head to watch the train)
would half-rise, let her morning paper slide
unheeded to the floor if he glide down
this rail embankment, kneel before her,
cloak cascading folds of heavenly silk?

But see how full of hope these little roads
that lead off towards the highway, writhing past
each fence, avoiding every obstacle
of debris, slicing every stagnant pool
of water. See, beyond the Council Depot
with its rows of pylon, miles of metal wire,
and twists and coils of plastic tubing, see
how flowers array themselves like Solomon
 and how the grass again begins to spread
its yellow carpet. See, God never did
discover how to spare His Godliness.

Cats patrol the sidings, sleeping dogs
curl up on mattresses, a man yawns
on the tailboard of a truck, waiting.
Life undisguised has words for all
would read this speeding landscape carefully
and see the angel come again, this time
not stepped from Heaven sumptuously apparelled,
but clad in early morning's simple clothing,
rising through the fret and discard of our lives
with gift of one more day to find the truth
of what we are and make it map and compass
for whatever roads are left our journeying.

PART V

"and suddenly the sun again..."

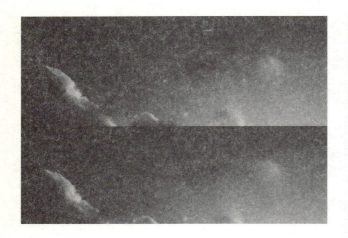

Scientists say planet could be 'Earthlike'

By Dennis Overbye

The most enticing property yet found outside our solar system is about 20 light years away in the constellation Libra, a team of European astronomers has announced.

The astronomers said Tuesday that they had discovered a planet five times as massive as the Earth orbiting a dim red star known as Gliese 581.

It is the smallest of the 200 or so planets that are known to exist outside of our solar system, the extrasolar, or exo-, planets. It orbits its home star within the habitable zone where surface water, the staff of life, could exist if other conditions are right, said Stéphane Udry of the Geneva Observatory.

"We are at the right place for that," said Udry, lead author of a paper describing the discovery, which has been submitted to the journal Astronomy & Astrophysics.

But he and other astronomers cautioned that it was far too soon to conclude that liquid water was there without more observations. Sara Seager, a planet expert at the Massachusetts Institute of Technology, said: "For example, if the planet had an atmosphere more massive than Venus's, then the surface would likely be too hot for liquid water."

Nevertheless, the discovery in the Gliese 581 system, where a Neptune-size planet was discovered two years ago and a planet of eight Earth masses is now suspected, catapults that system to the top of the list for future generations of space missions.

"On the treasure map of the universe, one would be tempted to mark this planet with an X," said Xavier Delfosse, a member of the team from Grenoble University in France, according to a news release from the European Southern Observatory, a multinational collaboration in Garching, Germany.

Dimitar Sasselov of the Harvard-Smithsonian Center for Astrophysics, who studies the structure and formation of planets, said: "It's 20 light years. We can go there."

100

January and How to Hold Her

at Collins' Bridge, The Royal Canal,
near Leixlip, Co. Kildare

One of those old masters who delights
in scrawny hedges and ploughed fields
was out this morning with his sketch-block,

stripped this narrow bridge to its essentials
leaving just enough to launch the eye
across long broken strokes that mark

where blade cut into clay. Then pencil points
betokening early birds, scuffed grey
on grey for clouds and mountains and then later

when he stood before the easel, head down,
straining back for January and how
to hold her — Pulled a stool up close and took

a tiny brush and pinched the sable tip
between his thumb and finger, draped a lace
of snow across the mountains and , for those

must eke their lives out on the margins
of the canvas, carefully touched the bridge
with one or two stick figures. Delicately.

Hotel Room, Easter

(after Edward Hopper)

I never sleep through mornings. I awaken
early to the daily possibility
of a new beginning. It could happen here

in this hotel room: solitary picture
(reproduction: New Orleans Plums,
by Hooker, 1819), and a wardrobe

with my single change of clothes. Unlike
the sprawling soldiery at the tomb I never
sleep through mornings, and especially

this morning it is written there will be
a new beginning more than usual
with mornings. It is said: a resurrection.

On Grafton Street It's Sidling into Summer

(remembering Chris Daybell, poet)

On Grafton Street it's sidling into summer and I think of you
and what we lost when you were lost to us — Your love of
                                      Beaudelaire,
Fellini — That late night we sat long past the last bus out of town
discussing them — Well, you discussing them. Me listening.

I think how many I have seen go down the wooded slope and take
with them so many irreplaceables: this one's turn of hand
and nimble step, or that one's ready wit and sharp ironic twist
of phrase would suddenly convert a simple story into Drama.

I'm always half-expecting I might see you, especially now this street
is sliding into summer and the flower-sellers are ablaze
with colour and the girls are leaving off their coats and I am walking
through the space you used to stand in on this corner selling poetry.

Inside me, where my lost have left an impress of themselves
                                        set down
in odd indelible moments, we are always in that fast-food
                                        restaurant
on Grafton Street, discussing Fellini's *'La Strada'* and Anthony
                                        Quinn. 'Genius,
only genius', you told me, 'can take brutality and turn it into art'.

Elegy for the Philadelphia Wireman (d. 1982?)

His work was found by chance one trash night
in a Philadelphia sidestreet by
a someone wasn't looking for it—
Dead, or moved away, the wireman
left no forwarding address, just
these twelve hundred pieces made
from discards, twisted, bent, persuaded
to yield something of the soul
they never had until his hands
pressed down on them and woke it:

skeletal umbrellas, batteries, pens
and nuts and bolts and wardrobe hangers,
coils of red and black electric cable
writhing skyward— Gesturing
despair? Or supplicating mercy? This
the art, the making of the thing,
the thing allowed to speak its heart,
without the artist intervening (and
no photographs, no anecdotes, no
long explanatory notes). This

the art, the what-remains-behind
to be the sole begetter of itself,
its poor creator gone to meet his own,
bequeathing this the most the valuable
the artefact could ever hope for:
absence of its maker and
the freedom to be beautiful despite
his uglinesses, wise despite
his crass stupidities, exemplar
of the kindnesses he knew a lifetime

hopelessly locked up inside him and
could show out only in these tapestries
and loops of interwoven wire,
these nails, these coins, these watches, tools
and jewellery bound by rubber bands
and tape. And even then could show out
only if we found them in that skip
before the trashmen took it. Even then
and only if we weren't looking for them.
Only if we found them just by chance.

Physics Today

*(remembering a teaching colleague
William Galland Stuart)*

Physics today (the Higher Paper)
and here we are together three
full hours to farther our careers,
explore the nature of our spot
in space, push out new frontiers, go
where man has not set foot before.

Physics today and only the sounds
of fingertips on calculators,
biros racing, a chair that creaks,
an occasional cough, an anxious sigh -
A pencil accidentally plunging
towards the centre of the earth.

And breathing (such fragility!).
And the feeling that time itself
has disentangled out from clocks
and watches, spread itself lengthwise
for minute examination. Question:
What is the nature of Time
in relation to light and friction? Answer?

Physics today. And we take our pens
and tackle with divine impertinence
considerations such as mass,
density and momentum, while outside
sky and wind and (can't you hear it?)
hum of gravity, swish of orbits
as we canter around the universe.

Gliese 581c

("On the treasure map of the universe, one would be tempted to mark this planet with an X" —news report)

Every time a animal thought extinct
becomes revealed on hidden camera
along his ancient pathways deep within
the jungles where few humans dare to stray
I'm broken by the heavy certainty
that, come tomorrow, he'll be hunted down.

Remember Cajamarca and the slaughter
of the Inca and all his hapless braves?
And Tumbes, where the virgins dedicated
to the Emperor were raped at will?
Such was our joy at finding a New World
we set about immediately to destroy it.

Now we have discovered a distant planet
like our own, at just the distance needed
from its star to harbour life. And graphs
are drawn, and speculation's rife about
our reaching through the 20 light-year barrier
that God has thrown across our greed.

Remember too the North American plains
and how we tamed them with our Iron Horse?
Brought Christianity to their savage peoples,
and then guns and whiskey, shot their buffalo
for sport, and then shot them and stole their land.
We're like a vicious medieval plague

that sweeps through countrysides, lays villages waste.
Remember too the veldts of Africa
fenced off, and every native killed we caught
inside the wire? — Remember the plantations
where the slaves who couldn't reach the quota
had their hands chopped off above the wrist?

Gliese 581c (for so we've named you),
I pray that God's distrust that started when
Eve ate the apple will continue, His
vast interstellar space protect you,
never see your peoples crowd your shores
to welcome gifts of coloured beads, and death.

'Entre Sardana i Sardana'

From the painting 'Between Sardana and Sardana'
by Xavier Nogues (1940). 1873-1941, at the
Museu de Montserrat, Abadia de Montserrat, Spain

The band is drawing breath, the clarinet
is laid aside, the flautist and the bass
are sipping drinks, the waitresses are busy
and the tables full of noisy talk.

Two young men lean up against a tree,
another stands somewhat apart. It's he
(there's always one) who chats the girls that pass—
Already one of his jocose remarks

has turned the heads of two young women walking
by. Their look is pitying— And they walk
straight past him, affecting to ignore him, but
he knows he made them look, and that's a start.

A little to the foreground there's a girl
sits with a quiet company but
wistfully looks towards another group
because her table seems a little dull.

That other group includes a few young men,
their heads together confidentially
across their drinks, their conversation serious
but full of smiles as well. Behind this bunch,

beneath the trees, a very angry lady
folds her arms and frowns and looks away
and will not be placated by the man
who opens out his hands imploringly.

And here's a waitress, apron neatly tied
around an even neater waist, who scans
the company for those who ordered this
bright tray of drinks she balances expertly.

Whoever owns them better claim them now
because the band is striking up again
to play another Sardana much too filled
with twists and turns to countenance sitting around!—

Those haughty girls who threw those pitying glances
now step out with those same boys— The third,
(he of the saucy word) leads out that girl
who seemed a trifle bored. That angry lady,

still a little sullen, has given in—
No one sits out Sardanas! Nobody
resists the irresistible!—This
kaleidoscope of whirling shirts and dresses!!

Mastermind

The Panama Canal was opened when? —
Correct. Who wrote the novel Lorna Doone? —
Correct. The 'H' in W.H.Auden? — Correct.
The date of your demise? Or is it true
about The Glorious Resurrection? — Pass.
Or what will happen when the oil runs out?
Or clean water? Or breathable air? And have we
neighbours circling some nearby star? — Pass.

And of what we have we loose the having
of it daily, without noticing —
The sacred waters of Lake Titicaca
are yearly in retreat and Greenland's glaciers
are collapsing — Nothing stays! It's therefore
that I have this yearning to be certain
in some special field or narrow sphere
or recondite pursuit, acknowledged expert

could be called upon to testify
in language axiomatic and exact
the truth and nothing but the truth — Someone
whose name alone attached to deposition,
proposition, premise would admit
no fallibility or doubt — Someone
whose word alone delivered in the midst
of argument would silence all dissent.

Meanwhile I'll answer questions on the novels
of Charles Dickens. Or on the types of popcorn
sold in cineplexes nationwide
from nineteen eighty-eight to the present day —
Or anything. As long as I can say
I know an everything about a something
I can feel my hand on the eternal —
I can feel I own a piece of God.

An Italian Wedding

San Marino's sunshine was confetti
on the Pianella when you stood
your extra-large American womanhood
against the nearest statue, shouting: "Now!

Take me now! Come on!" But all unknown
to you I stepped out all unknown to me
into your photograph, my hand in yours
colliding, you and I forever wed

on cellophane, together bedded down
between sea-views of Miremare,
our embrace discovered only when
the picture albums circulate with laughter

and the after-dinner cigarettes:
"And who's this guy; for Gawd's sakes?!" — They
will never understand our timeless union,
they will never understand... But why

go on like this? Unmistakably
a New World Girl of centrefold
dimensions, you. And I? —Another stunted
European who knows you'll find a way

to cancel out our Instamatic courtship
leaving just the faintest smudge to show
what might have been. Yes, for you my spirit
flies the wide Atlantic, nightly, searching, searching, searching...

There is an Hour of Night

There is an hour of night the globe slows down
just short of stop, the spheres begin the task
of realignment, inclination, and
those pivotal necessities of time
before another day allowed to dawn.

This hour is weighed the mouse's step, is gauged
the swing of shutter, flap of tablecloth,
the whisper of the door unlatched. This hour
will raise along the nape of memory
the strands will plait the present with the past

until - like comb that's whirred by fingernail -
a gap defines a loss, ignites a pain
again, a shout that echoes silently
in this still quietude of stars and dark
and troubled sleep. This hour begins again

the salving of the wound that never healed,
the strapping tight of fractures of the psyche,
while God's own engineers check out the cables,
test the fuses, calculate the astral
combinations, switch the power back on.

And morning glows along the curtain's hem.

Springtime at the Zoo

It's springtime at the zoo and all
of animal life is here. Raunchy
rabbits populate pet's corner,
lizards chase their tails while she
in khaki shorts & top , takes him
while he holds himself erect
beside the bull seal.

It's springtime at the zoo and all
of animal life is here. Monkeys
upside-down expose themselves
behind his back while he struggles
with the camera, and she stands
impatiently waiting to be taken
beside the pink flamingos.

First Green Shoots

I read a politician has been criticised
for saying that she sees the first green shoots
arriving to signal the end of the Recession.

Just this morning I saw several blades
as green as any banknote scything from
the winter burial mound that is my garden.

There is of course a cycle of the seasons
that passeth understanding more than those
Financial Products we devised, and yet

more comprehensible than the downward spirals
of the ISAQ and the NYSE and the suits
on talk shows trying to explain in detail

how they got it wrong (Great help!). Secularist
I am, but glad that they were not in charge
when Nature judged it time again to give us

this New Year, new made. It's great that she,
and only she, has got the say on how
and when to let the first green shoots appear.

And it's great that she is regulated
by the Regulator and that His,
and only His, terms and conditions apply.

The Dark Side of the Earth

Morning in the park. Is there
a paradise could better this?
The trees stand innocent of storm,
the pathways run untrodden over
bridges — Everything is fresh
from re-creation overnight.

The gardener salutes me, spade
a flash of light across his shoulder.
Watching from my usual seat
I see the playground slides reflect
the sun. I hear the River Griffeen
tumbling, laughing like a child.

Morning in the park. I watch him
search the flowerbeds, probe, until —
inevitable the moment! — he will
slice his blade into the clay,
dislodge the worm and weed, reveal
the dark side of the earth.

Sudden Rainshower

The sudden slant of it, the sudden
sheesh of it, the thousand million
crashes of it on windowpane and pavement,
tarpaulin and plastic-covered
supermarket trolley-bay
where people rush to shelter squealing,
stumbling, cursing, laughing. Then

the sudden heavy smell of wet cement,
brown outdoor-chairs-on-sale now
suddenly browner, and the sudden pools,
the gutters suddenly alive and then
the sudden silence when the sabres stop
and everyone is breathless taking in
what He can do without a by-your-leave.

And suddenly the sun again.